The Lion of Judah
in Never-Never Land

The Lion of Judah in Never-Never Land

The Theology of C. S. Lewis Expressed
in His Fantasies for Children

by

KATHRYN ANN LINDSKOOG

WILLIAM B. EERDMANS PUBLISHING COMPANY
Grand Rapids, Michigan

TO MARILYN PEPPIN,
A GREAT FRIEND OF NARNIA,
AND TO JOHN, CHARLES,
AND RICHARD TURECEK
IN HOPES THAT THEY MAY SOMEDAY
BECOME THE SAME.

48078

Preface

At about the age of six, C. S. Lewis invented the imaginary world of "Animal-Land" or "Boxen", as it later came to be called, and over the next few years he wrote numerous stories and histories about the "dressed animals" which inhabited it. Though it is remarkable that a boy could write so well and could sustain a single story for over a hundred pages in an exercise book, the "Chronicles of Boxen" (as yet unpublished) are marred by a conscious effort on the young Lewis's part to make them "grown up" — which to him meant stodgy, prosaic, and political. What makes this so ironic is that Lewis's favourite books were fairy tales and romances. He was ashamed of these tastes, however, and in smothering his sense of wonder under the overlay of Boxen newspapers and railway timetables, his literary proclivities were — if not wasted — at least misdirected. There is a good deal of humour in these early efforts, but just at the moment when the humour seems likely to bubble over and turn the stories in the direction they seem to *want* to take, Lewis brings them under the control of his even greater desire to make them dull and "believable". Lewis told me that during his childhood "real" books meant, not the kind he enjoyed, but those that reflected most nearly the conversations and interests of adults. In short, his talents went into the writing of what *he* thought "purely human" stories.

The interest in Boxen faded out by the time Lewis was thirteen (1911), to be replaced by a keen interest in poetry. Whereas Boxen represented the sober, workaday idea he had of life, his early poems reflect the favourite theme of all his later writings — the romantic yearning after transcendent joy. Another thing they reflect is Lewis's move from Christianity to atheism. As Lewis himself said of this period in his life: "The two hemispheres of my mind were in the sharpest contrast. On the one side a many-islanded sea of poetry and myth; on the other a glib and shallow 'rationalism'. Nearly all that I loved I believed to be imaginary; nearly all that I believed to be real I thought grim and meaningless."[1]

A particularly unpleasant result of his loss of Faith is that Lewis became ambitious —

---

[1]*Surprised by Joy.* London, 1955, ch. xi.

greedy for a niche in this world. Though poetry remained his great love, Lewis still had hopes of writing an "adult" novel. There are references in his letters and papers to books he began but never finished. The longest fragment which has survived, written in about 1927, consists of the first two chapters of a novel about a young English doctor's visit to Belfast to see his Irish relàtions. It is ample proof that Lewis was still half-enamoured of the bustling, enterprising, "real" life of the men of his father's generation. Of the crew aboard the overnight boat from Liverpool to Belfast, his hero "Dr Easley" says: "I feel I cannot describe these Ulstermen better than by saying that they realized perfectly a child's dream of what a 'grown up' ought to be. Their hands were hairy and massive: their movements and voices were sudden, confident and practical: they moved to an incessant jingling of money, flapping of watch chains. . . . They wore the uniforms of respectability." This is not satire. In seeking some replacement for the Faith which he had lost, Lewis found much that was homely and comfortable in the only world in which he believed.

This was probably the last "purely human" novel Lewis ever attempted to write. In 1931 he was converted to Christianity and his world was turned inside out. He discovered in the Eternal Son of God the Object of all his yearning and, from the perspective afforded by this discovery, he saw man in a totally new light. Nowhere in his writings is this perspective better summed up than in his sermon "The Weight of Glory", in which he says: "Nations, cultures, arts, civilizations — these are mortal and their life is to ours as the life of a gnat. But it is immortals whom we joke with, work with, marry, snub, and exploit — immortal horrors or everlasting splendours. This does not mean that we are to be perpetually solemn. We must play. But our merriment must be of that kind (and it is, in fact, the merriest kind) which exists between people who have, from the outset, taken each other seriously."[2]

This new angle of vision, which left Lewis both more serious and a great deal merrier, had several interesting effects on the books he wrote afterwards. Firstly, the term "purely human" could never mean to him so earthbound and limited a thing as it does to most non-believers. No, take it or leave it, men are, and always have been, inextricably bound up with the acts of God and the infinite stakes for which life is played. (Contrast this with the truncated "reality" of most modern novelists, for whom sex is the best, and death the worst, thing that can happen to a man.) Secondly,

[2]*The Weight of Glory and Other Addresses.* New York, 1949, p. 15.

before his conversion, when Lewis cared desperately about securing fame through literature, he found little to write about. When the most real thing was to become the least real thing in God's plan for men, his genius broke free. When he ceased trying to *make* books come, they gushed forth. Looking back on it some years later, he said: "I have never exactly 'made' a story. With me the process is much more like bird-watching than like either talking or building. I see *pictures* . . . a whole set might join themselves so consistently that there you had a complete story: without doing anything yourself."[3] Thirdly, having escaped from the narrow and tiresome confines of "adult reality", Lewis was able to see the world with the unclouded wonder and excitement of a child.

Real children may have had some part to play in this. At the outbreak of the Second World War several schoolgirls were evacuated to Lewis's home on the outskirts of Oxford. Lewis had no experience of children, and writing to his brother (who was in France) on 18 September 1939, he said that though the young evacuees were "nice, unaffected creatures" they kept asking "What shall we do now?"

I don't know what part Lewis played in the

---

[3]"On Three Ways of Writing for Children", *Of Other Worlds,* ed. by Walter Hooper. New York, 1967, p. 32.

entertainment of the young visitors, but they almost certainly provided the impetus for what are now his most popular books. On the back of a manuscript of another book he was writing at this time, I found this solitary paragraph: "This book is about four children whose names were Ann, Martin, Rose and Peter. But it is most about Peter who was the youngest. They all had to go away from London suddenly because of the Air Raids, and because Father, who was in the army, had gone off to the War and Mother was doing some kind of war work. They were sent to stay with a relation of Mother's who was a very old Professor who lived by himself in the country."

It is not known whether Lewis wrote any more of the story at this time. The first complete draft of it — which contained no mention of the great Lion, Aslan — was finished by March 1949. Possibly because Lewis had been having a good many dreams about lions at the time, Aslan suddenly came bounding into it, and by December 1949 Lewis had completed the first Chronicle of Narnia — *The Lion, the Witch and the Wardrobe*. More "pictures" began forming in Lewis's head, and the next two stories, *Prince Caspian* and *The Voyage of the "Dawn Treader"*, were completed by the end of February 1950. Before the year was out he had written *The Silver Chair* and *The*

Horse and His Boy and made a start on *The Magician's Nephew*. The final installment, *The Last Battle,* was written two years later.

These seven fairy stories were an instant success with children, for whom they were ostensibly written. Parents read them to find out what all the "fuss" was about, became converted, and pressed them on their friends. The books are now selling over a million copies a year and — a recent sign of their popularity — hard-up college students will run up enormous book-bills in order to give copies away. Lewis was a master story-teller with an uncanny visual imagination, and this is probably the simplest explanation as to why the books give so much pleasure. Another reason for their success is what is popularly referred to as the books' "many levels of meaning" (By placing his adventures in fairyland, beyond contamination by our usual prejudices, Lewis catches us off guard and helps us to attend to things which matter most in this world. By degrees which are often unnoticed by even the most cautious atheist, we progress from a love of Narnia, to a greater love of Aslan himself, to a sharp regret that there is no Aslan in this world, to a sudden recognition which makes the heart sing that there *is* an Aslan in this world — and then, if my own experience is any guide — Narnia and this world interlock and Aslan and Christ are seen as one.)

I think we are ill-advised to short-circuit this process by handing these books to children with a string of explanations about who is what. The books do this so much more effectively on their own. Most adult Christians will, however, realize that there is a great deal of theology behind the Narnian Chronicles, and Mrs. Lindskoog's book is an attempt to show us what that theology is. It is certainly better that we should know it than not.

Lewis believed that good books should always be read many times. I have never met anyone who had read his Narnian stories only once, and if Lewis were alive this is the story I should most want to tell him. A few years ago I learned of a family here in Oxford who, one Sunday afternoon, finished reading their little boy *The Lion, the Witch and the Wardrobe* — the adventure which begins with four children finding their way into Narnia through the back of a wardrobe. While the parents were having tea downstairs, such a terrible racket began upstairs they thought the house was falling in. They rushed up to find their son with a hatchet. He had smashed through the back of his parents' wardrobe and was hacking away at the wall behind it. I'm told that the only way to save the house was to read him another story of Narnia.

Oxford, England   WALTER HOOPER

Contents

[15]

. . . though I thought not of Thee under the form of a human body, yet was I constrained to image Thee to be something corporeal in space, either infused into the world, or infinitely diffused beyond it . . . since whatsoever I conceived, deprived of this space, appeared as nothing to me, yea, altogether nothing, not even a void. . . .

St. Augustine, The Confessions

These things which are said of God and other things are predicted neither unequivocally nor equivocally, but analogically. . . . Accordingly, since we arrive at the knowledge of God from other things, the reality of the names predicated of God and other things is first in God according to His mode, but the meaning of the name is on Him afterwards. Wherefore He is said to be named from His effects.

St. Thomas Aquinas, Summa contra Gentiles

As to Aslan's other name, well, I want you to guess. Has there never been anyone in this *world who (1) Arrived at the same time as Father Christmas (2) Said he was the Son of the Great Emperor (3) Gave himself up for someone else's fault to be jeered at and killed by wicked people (4) Came to life again (5) Is sometimes spoken of as a Lamb (at the end of the "Dawn Treader")? Don't you really know His name in this world?*

C. S. Lewis, A Letter to an American Girl

Chapter One

Making Pictures

— Images of God —

"To forbid the making of pictures about God would be to forbid thinking about God at all, for man is so made that he has no way to think except in pictures." Thus Dorothy Sayers states the premise underlying the pictorial symbolism used by C. S. Lewis in his delightful series of children's books, *The Chronicles of Narnia.* She continues with the broader assertion that all language about everything is analogical and that we think in a series of metaphors. We can explain nothing in terms of itself, but only in terms of other things.[1]

Lewis himself, in his book *Miracles,* refutes attempts to conceive of God without the use of metaphorical images:

---

[1]*The Mind of the Maker* (New York: Harcourt, Brace, 1941), p. 22.

'I don't believe in a personal God', says one, 'but I do believe in a great spiritual force.' What he has not noticed is that the word 'force' has let in all sorts of images about winds and tides and electricity and gravitation. 'I don't believe in a personal God', says another, 'but I do believe we are all parts of one great Being which moves and works through us all' — not noticing that he has merely exchanged the image of a fatherly and royal-looking man for the image of some widely extended gas or fluid. A girl I knew was brought up by 'higher thinking' parents to regard God as a perfect 'substance'; in later life she realized that this had actually led her to think of Him as something like a vast tapioca pudding. (To make matters worse, she disliked tapioca.) We may feel ourselves quite safe from this degree of absurdity, but we are mistaken. If a man watches his own mind, I believe he will find that what profess to be specially advanced or philosophic conceptions of God are, in his thinking always accompanied by vague images which, if inspected, would turn out to be even more absurd than the man-like images aroused by Christian theology.[2]

But the Christian doctrine of God is not the only concept embodied in the Narnia tales. Lewis has subtly and intricately woven into them a variety of Christian doctrines — though

---

[2]New York: Macmillan, 1947, pp. 90-91.

of course religious concepts are secondary to Lewis's first concern, a rollicking good story. Readers are more than welcome to miss the Christian teaching — at least on the conscious level.

The doctrines fall into three main categories: Lewis's concept of nature — the system of all phenomena in space and time; Lewis's concept of God — the creator, redeemer, and sustainer of nature and mankind; and Lewis's concept of man in his relationship to nature, God, and his fellow man. The basis of these concepts is neither fundamentalism nor modernism, but Lewis's particular Christian orthodoxy, which Chad Walsh has termed Classical Christianity.[3]

— Lewis's Childhood Writing —

Before seeking out Lewis's Christian beliefs in his books for children, one might consider the nature of these fantasies. Lewis claimed to write the kind of books he himself liked to read. Hence it is not surprising that his stories for children contain the subject matter that interested him as a child.

His early literary tastes are clearly recalled in the autobiographical story of his conversion, *Surprised by Joy*. Here he tells us that he had soon staked out a claim to one of the attics

---

[3]*C. S. Lewis, Apostle to Skeptics* (New York: Macmillan, 1949), p. 171.

and made it "his study." It was in this little retreat that his first stories were written, and illustrated, with enormous satisfaction. They were an attempt to combine his two chief literary pleasures, "dressed animals" and courtly "knights-in-armour." As early as his sixth, seventh, and eighth years, the mood of the systematizer was already strong in him. This led from romancing to historiography — he set about writing a full history of "Animal-Land," complete with a map and colorful illustrations created from his paint box.[4]

Lewis's continued regard for geography is apparent in his Narnian series, as well as in his literary criticism. Of William Morris's romances he once said, "Other stories have only scenery; his have geography."[5] That evaluation can be applied to his own stories as well.

Although the fairy tales he wrote as an adult contain the same emphasis upon knights in armor, history, and geography as characterized his youthful efforts, Lewis is quick to emphasize the major difference between the two. Of the former, he depreciatively comments: "My invented world was full (for me) of interest, bustle, humour, and character; but there was

[4]*Surprised by Joy* (London: Geoffrey Bles, 1955), pp. 19-20.
[5]Charles A. Brady, "Introduction to Lewis," *America,* June 10, 1944, p. 269.

no poetry, even no romance in it. It was almost astonishingly prosaic." He notes: "For readers of my children's books, the best way of putting this would be to say that Animal-Land had nothing whatever in common with Narnia except the anthropomorphic beasts. Animal-Land, by its whole quality, excluded the least hint of wonder."[6]

As a child, Lewis had not yet acquired the Christian Romanticism[7] which motivates his Narnian tales and distinguishes them from the earlier fantasies. The Narnian tales seem to illustrate the assertion of J. R. R. Tolkien that "the Gospels contain a fairy-story, or a story of a larger kind which embraces all the essence of fairy-stories." The Gospels "contain many marvels — peculiarly artistic, beautiful, and mov-

---

[6]*Surprised by Joy*, p. 22.

[7]In describing Charles Williams as a Christian romantic, Lewis states: "A romantic theologian does not mean one who is romantic about theology but one who is theological about romance, one who considers the theological implications of those experiences which are called romantic. The belief that the most serious and ecstatic experiences either of human love or of imaginative literature have such theological implications, and that they can be healthy and fruitful only if the implications are diligently thought out and severely lived, is the principle of all his work" — "Preface," *Essays Presented to Charles Williams*, ed. C. S. Lewis (Grand Rapids, Michigan: Eerdmans, 1966), p. vi.

ing: 'mythical' in their perfect, self-contained significance; and at the same time powerfully symbolic and allegorical; and among the marvels is the greatest and most complete conceivable eucatastrophe," the Birth of Christ. "The Resurrection is the eucatastrophe of the story of the Incarnation."[8]

According to Tolkien,

> there is no tale ever told that men would rather find was true, and none which so many skeptical men have accepted as true on its own merits. . . . To reject it leads either to sadness or to wrath. It is not difficult to imagine the peculiar excitement and joy that one would feel if any specially beautiful fairy story were found to be 'primarily' true, its narrative to be history, without thereby necessarily losing the mythical or allegorical significance that it had possessed. . . . The Christian joy, the *Gloria,* is of the same kind. . . ."[9]

Although the child Lewis was not yet acquainted with these concepts, he had experienced that undefinable desire, that romantic longing, referred to by German poets as *Sehnsucht*. This is obvious in the imaginative preoccupations of his childhood: "I wish I had

[8]"On Fairy Stories," *Essays Presented to Charles Williams,* p. 83.
[9]"On Fairy Stories," pp. 83-84.

time to tell you of all the other constructions — the unknown room in the house which
one was always hoping to discover, the chess
men coming alive as in *Alice,* the garden which
was partly in the West and partly in the
past. . . ."[10]

— The Narnian Series —

These very elements of subject are present
in the Narnian Chronicles, along with richly
romantic settings and details. Lewis defends
this literary mode with a commentary on the
contrasting approach of T. S. Eliot:

> Mr. Eliot may succeed in persuading the
> reading youth of England to have done with
> robes of purple and pavements of marble. But
> he will not therefore find them walking in
> sackcloth on floors of mud — he will only
> find them in smart, ugly suits walking on rub-
> beroid. It has all been tried before. The older
> Puritans took away the maypoles and the
> mince-pies: but they did not bring in the
> millennium, they only brought in the Restora-
> tion. If Mr. Eliot disdains the eagles and
> trumpets of epic poetry because the fashion of

---

[10]C. S. Lewis, "Psychoanalysis and Literary Criticism,"
Essays and Studies, XXVII (1942), 18. Also available
in *They Asked for a Paper* (London: Geoffrey Bles,
1962), pp. 120-138; and in *Selected Literary Essays,*
ed. Walter Hooper (London: Cambridge, 1969),
pp. 286-300.

this world passes away, I honour him. But if he goes on to draw the conclusion that all poetry should have the penitential qualities of his own best work, I believe he is mistaken. As long as we live in merry middle earth it is necessary to have middle things.[11]

In accordance with this position, Lewis's children's books employ both the trumpets and eagles of epic poetry and simple merriment. They glorify such epic scenes as "that wonderful hall with the ivory roof and the west door all hung with peacock's feathers and the eastern door which opens right onto the sea"[12] and also idealize the more "middle" domesticities such as taking tea in a clean little cave. "And really it was a wonderful tea. There was a nice brown egg, lightly boiled, for each of them, and then sardines on toast. . . ."[13]

Whether grand or trivial, every scene in the Narnian series is colored by *Faërie*. According to Tolkien, "Faërie . . . may perhaps most nearly be translated by Magic — but is magic of a peculiar mood and power, at the furthest pole from the vulgar devices of the laborious, scientific magician."[14] Indeed, this type of magi-

[11]*A Preface to Paradise Lost* (London: Oxford, 1942), p. 133.
[12]C. S. Lewis, *The Lion, the Witch and the Wardrobe* (New York: Macmillan, 1950), p. 148.
[13]*Ibid.*, p. 11.
[14]"On Fairy Stories," p. 43.

cian is thoroughly ridiculed by Lewis in *The Magician's Nephew*. Lewis's Faërie, agreeing with Tolkien's definition,[15] "contains many things besides elves and fays, and besides dwarfs, witches, trolls, giants, or dragons: it holds the seas, the sun, the moon, the sky; and the earth, and all things that are in it: tree and bird, water and stone, wine and bread, and ourselves, mortal men, when we are enchanted." The heart of the desire of Faërie is fantasy, the making or glimpsing of Other-worlds.[16]

According to G. K. Chesterton, whom Lewis credits as greatly clarifying Christianity for him,[17] "The only right way of telling a story is to begin at the beginning — at the beginning of the world. Therefore all books have to be begun in the wrong way for the sake of brevity."[18]

Lewis's story begins in the first book at the time when London children were evacuated to the country during the Second World War. The four Pevensie children, boarding at a country estate, find their way through an old wardrobe into the land of Narnia. Their adventures there lead into three other books of the same scheme, that of children from this world transported by magic into a world of fairy-tale creatures be-

---

[15]*Ibid.*, p. 42.

[16]*Ibid.*, p. 63.

[17]*Surprised by Joy*, p. 210.

[18]G. K. Chesterton, *William Blake* (London: Duckworth, 1910), p. 1.

longing to a great lion. The fifth book is the tale of two native children of that world who also are chosen by the great Lion to serve the land of Narnia and to know him in a special way.

Only in the sixth book does Lewis begin at the beginning — at the beginning of the world of Narnia. The intrusion of two Victorian children into that newborn world begins the complications which give rise to all the later adventures. In the seventh and last book of the series these events are culminated in the end of the world of Narnia.[19]

Each of these adventures, although complete in itself, opens doors to many other possible accounts of episodes in the history of Narnia. Each is written in the tone of George Mac-Donald,[20] at the conclusion of his book *The Princess and the Goblin:*

---

[19]Thus the chronological order of the books by events is as follows:

The Magician's Nephew (1955)
The Lion, the Witch and the Wardrobe (1950)
The Horse and His Boy (1954)
Prince Caspian (1951)
The Voyage of the "Dawn Treader" (1952)
The Silver Chair (1953)
The Last Battle (1956)

[20]"I regarded him as my master; indeed I fancy I have never written a book in which I did not quote from him" — C. S. Lewis, *George MacDonald* (New York: Macmillan, 1954), p. 20.

"— But there! I don't mean to go any farther at present."

"Then you're leaving the story unfinished, Mr. Author!"

"Not more unfinished than a story ought to be, I hope. If you ever know a story finished, all I can say is I never did. Somehow, stories won't finish. I think I know why, but I won't say that either, now."[21]

Tolkien refers to George MacDonald in his analysis of types of fairy stories, stating that fairy stories as a whole have three faces: "the Mystical towards the Supernatural; the Magical towards Nature; and the Mirror of scorn and pity towards Man." Of course, the essential face of Faërie is the Magical one. If the others appear at all, the degree is variable and may be decided by the individual storyteller. "The Magical, the fairy-story, may be used as a *Mirour de l'Omme;* and it may (but not so easily) be made a vehicle of Mystery. This at least is what George MacDonald attempted. . . ."[22]

Apparently C. S. Lewis has followed MacDonald's example. As seen in the résumé of his fairy stories, this series is fragmentary. Yet each book is a vehicle of mystery. There is a strong unity of philosophy and consistency of

---

[21]New York: Macmillan, 1926, p. 267.
[22]"On Fairy Stories," p. 53.

doctrine throughout the collection of whimsical episodes — Lewis's concepts of nature, of God, and of human life.

Chapter Two

Spoiled Goodness: Lewis's Concept of Nature

— Rural Beauty —

Lewis's appreciation of geographical land-
scape is what one would expect of a Christian
romantic — a reverent and insatiable delight.
In his personal account, he relates:

> What the real garden had failed to do, the
> toy garden did. It made me aware of nature
> — not, indeed, as a storehouse of forms and
> colours but as something cool, dewy, fresh,
> exuberant. . . . As long as I live my imagina-
> tion of Paradise will retain something of my
> brother's toy garden.[1]

Lewis's wonder at the fresh exuberance of
nature is expressed in his first description of the
real Narnia, as the great thaw occurs in *The*

---

[1]*Surprised by Joy*, p. 14.

Lion, the Witch and the Wardrobe. The sudden rejuvenation of the forest is recorded with great delicacy and sensuous detail. Finally, as the trees begin to come alive, the larches and birches in green, the laburnums in gold, a dwarf stops and announces with horror, "This is no thaw; this is spring" (pp. 97-98).

In contrast to this poignant presentation of nature approached with childlike eagerness is Lewis's short story "The Shoddy Lands," an adult fantasy. The shoddy lands are discovered upon an accidental journey into the mind of a frivolous young woman. There the scenery is extremely vague and dingy, each nondescript feature of the surrounding merely a crude, shabby apology for part of nature. There is no freshness, detail, or clarity, because the woman's mind is jaded and blasé.[2]

Again, at the opposite extreme, the rich profuseness of nature is sensuously exaggerated in Lewis's description of the Wood between the Worlds in *The Magician's Nephew:*

> You could almost feel the trees growing . . . a pool every few yards as far as his eyes could reach. You could almost feel the trees drinking the water up with their roots. This wood

---

[2]"The Shoddy Lands," *The Best from Fantasy and Science Fiction: Sixth Series* (New York: Doubleday, 1957), p. 159. Also available in *Of Other Worlds: Essays and Stories,* ed. Walter Hooper (London: Geoffrey Bles, 1966), pp. 99-106.

was very much alive. . . . It was a *rich* place: as rich as plum-cake.[3]

Here Lewis is apparently reverting to "the older conception of Nature . . . tingling with anthropomorphic life, dancing, ceremonial, a festival not a machine."[4] In an early poem, Lewis once said,

> Faeries must be in the woods
> Or the satyrs' laughing broods —
> Tritons in the summer sea,
> Else how could the dead things be
> Half so lovely as they are? . . .[5]

Later, Lewis developed this idea in lively prose in his introduction to D. E. Harding's *The Hierarchy of Heaven and Earth*. "We have emptied the baby out with the bath," he states. "In emptying out the dryads and the gods (which, admittedly, 'would not do' just as they stood) we appear to have thrown out the whole universe, ourselves included."[6] According to Lewis, a dryad is the abbreviated symbol for all

---

[3]New York: Macmillan, 1955, pp. 25-26.

[4]C. S. Lewis, *English Literature in the Sixteenth Century* (Oxford: Clarendon, 1954), p. 4. For Lewis's scholarly analysis of the history and uses of the word *nature,* read "Nature" in his book *Studies in Words* (London: Cambridge, 1960), pp. 24-74.

[5]Clive Hamilton [C. S. Lewis], "Song," *Spirits in Bondage* (London: William Heinemann, 1919), p. 73.

[6]New York: Harper, 1952, p. 12.

we know about trees. So is "mind or consciousness" a symbol for what we know about behavior. Rejection of these concepts occurs when the symbol is mistaken for the object.[7]

> At the outset the universe appears packed with will, intelligence, life and positive qualities; every tree is a nymph and every planet a god. Man himself is akin to the gods. The advance of knowledge gradually empties this rich and genial universe: first of its gods, then of its colours, smells, sounds, and tastes, finally of solidity itself as solidity was originally imagined. As those items are taken from the world, they are transferred to the subjective side of the account: classified as our sensations, thoughts, images or emotions. The Subject becomes gorged, inflated, at the expense of the Object. But the matter does not rest there. The same method which has emptied the world now proceeds to empty ourselves. The masters of the method soon announce that we were just as mistaken (and in much the same way) when we attributed 'souls' or 'selves' or 'minds' to human organisms, as when we attributed Dryads to the trees. Animism apparently begins at home. We, who have personified all other things, turn out to be ourselves mere personifications.[8]

---

[7]*Ibid.*, p. 12.
[8]*Ibid.*, p. 10.

The structure of Lewis's children's books is in direct opposition to the philosophy decried in this introduction.

— The Supernatural —

The Narnian series hinges upon the acceptance of supernatural phenomena:

> "Supposing I told you I'd been in a place where animals can talk and where there are — er — enchantments and dragons — and — well, all the sorts of things you have in fairy tales." Scrubb felt terribly awkward as he said this and got red in the face.
>
> "How did you get there?" said Jill. She also felt curiously shy.
>
> "The only way you can — by Magic," said Eustace almost in a whisper.[9]

There are, of course, skeptics in these books. In *The Lion, the Witch and the Wardrobe* the children did not accept Lucy's tale about discovering Narnia when they first heard it. They consulted the wise old professor about her strange story. They complained that when they looked in the wardrobe there was nothing there, asserting that if things are real they're there all the time. "Are they?" the Professor said. The time element also bothered the children. During less than one minute, Lucy claimed to have

---

[9] *The Silver Chair* (New York: Macmillan, 1953), p. 4.

spent several hours in Narnia. "That is the very thing that makes her story so likely to be true," said the Professor. He explained that if there really was a door in his house that led to some other world, it would be very likely that the other world had a separate time of its own so that however long one stayed there it would never take up any time on earth.

"But do you really mean, Sir," asked one of the boys, "that there could be other worlds — all over the place, just round the corner — like that?" (pp. 39-40).

When the children had had actual experiences with the supernatural, the concept of other worlds was much easier to accept. Once they had been out of their own world, they could conceive of many others with comparative facility. The idea came to Digory in *The Magician's Nephew:* "Why, if we can get back to our own world by jumping into *this* pool, mightn't we get somewhere else by jumping into one of the others? Supposing there was a world at the bottom of every pool!" (p. 30).

The philosophy underlying this structure of multiple natures is clearly explained in a speculative passage in *Miracles* (p. 20). Lewis begins with the supernaturalist's belief that a Primary Thing exists independently and has produced our composition of space, time, and connected events which we call nature. There might be other natures so created which we don't know about. Lewis is not referring here to other solar systems or galaxies existing far away in our own system of space and time, because those would be a part of our nature in spite of their distance. Only if other natures were not spatiotemporal at all, or if their space and time had no relation to our own, could we call them different natures. This is important in Lewis's literary theory:

> No merely physical strangeness or merely spatial distance will realize that idea of otherness which is what we are always trying to grasp in a story about voyaging through space: you must go into another dimension. To construct plausible and moving 'other worlds' you must draw on the only real 'other world' we know, that of the spirit.[10]

The only relationship to our system would be through common derivation from a single supernatural force. Here Lewis resorts to the figure of authorship discussed by Dorothy Sayers in *The Mind of the Maker*.[11] The only relationship between events in one novel and events in another is the fact that they were written by the same author, which causes a continuity in his mind only.

There could be no connection between the

---

[10]"On Stories," *Essays Presented to Charles Williams*, p. 98.
[11]*Miracles*, p. 118.

events in one nature and the events in another, by virtue of the character of the two systems. But perhaps God would choose to bring the two natures into partial contact at some point. This would not turn the two natures into one, because they would still lack the total reciprocity of one nature, and this spasmodic interlocking would arise, not from within them, but from a divine act. Thus, each of the two natures would be "supernatural" to the other. But in an even more absolute sense, their contact itself would be supernatural, because it would be not only outside of a particular nature but beyond any and every nature.[12]

When this philosophical speculation is geared to a childhood level of interests, delightful possibilities for story situations appear. One of these, the concept of our world being known elsewhere as a myth, is introduced by the prince of Narnia to his young English guest:

> "Do you mean to say," asked Caspian, "that you three come from a round world (round like a ball) and you've never told me! It's really too bad of you. Because we have fairy-tales in which there are round worlds and I always loved them. I never believed there were any real ones. But I've always wished there were and I've always longed to live in one. Oh, I'd give anything — I wonder why you can get into our world and we never

---

[12]*Ibid.*, p. 21.

get into yours? If only I had the chance! It must be exciting to live on a thing like a ball. Have you ever been to the parts where people walk about upside down?"

Edmund shook his head. "And it isn't like that," he added. "There's nothing particularly exciting about a round world when you're there."[13]

Just as our world bears aspects of a fairy-tale world from the Narnian point of view, so the Narnian world is rich with figures of earthly folklore. For example, there are giants, both good and bad. But they affect us in much the same way. "A *good* giant is legitimate: but he would be twenty tons of living, earth-shaking oxymoron. The intolerable pressure, the sense of something older, wilder, and more earthy than humanity, would still cleave to him."[14]

In Narnia, giants, centaurs, dryads, fauns, dwarfs, sea serpents, mermaids, dragons, monopods, and pirates live in an environment of castles, caves, magic whistles, golden chessmen, and enchanted gardens. The implication is that all elements of myth as we know them are shadows of a foreign reality. This idea is also demonstrated in Lewis's science fiction trilogy.[15]

---

[13]*The Voyage of the "Dawn Treader"* (New York: Macmillan, 1952), p. 195.
[14]Lewis, "On Stories," p. 95.
[15]*Out of the Silent Planet* (1938)
  Perelandra (1943)
  That Hideous Strength (1945)

— The Corruption of Nature —

C. S. Lewis is known for opposing the spirit of modern thought with the unpopular Christian doctrines of sin and evil. He considers evil not as a nebulous abstraction but as a destructive immanence which should be openly recognized and not complacently ignored, even though such recognition is disquieting. This principle is the major element in Lewis's otherwise happy concept of nature.[16] In his own words, "We find ourselves in a world of transporting pleasures, ravishing beauties, and tantalising possibilities, but all constantly being destroyed, all coming to nothing. Nature has all the air of a good thing spoiled."[17] In *The Magician's Nephew* original sin enters Narnia: ". . . before the new, clean world I gave you is seven hours old, a force of evil has already entered it; waked and brought hither by this son of Adam" (p. 121).

Throughout the rest of the series, this element of evil manifests itself in Narnia in various forms, always subjugating and trying to destroy the goodness in nature. In *The Lion, the Witch and the Wardrobe* the leader of evil forces is the White Witch, who has banished spring: ". . . it is she that has got all Narnia under her thumb. It's she that makes it always winter.

---

[16]Walsh, *C. S. Lewis, Apostle to Skeptics*, p. 81.
[17]*Miracles*, p. 147.

Always winter and never Christmas" (p. 14).

In *Prince Caspian* a wise old dwarf informs the Prince of the harm done by evil King Miraz, who has trampled out the natural beauty of Narnia. He assures the Prince that what he had heard about Old Narnia is true. "It is the country of Aslan, the country of the Waking Trees and Visible Naiads, of Fauns and Satyrs, of Dwarfs and Giants, of the gods and the Centaurs, of Talking Beasts"; but the wicked king no longer allows them to be spoken of.[18] This is the situation lamented by Lewis in an early lyric:

> The faerie people from our woods are gone,
> No Dryads have I found in all our trees.
> No Triton blows his horn about our seas
> And Arthur sleeps far hence in Avalon.[19]

In *The Silver Chair* another witch has assumed power, this time by suppression of the glad natural order of the world beneath the surface of the earth, reminiscent of Wagner's Nibelheim.[20] There she enchanted merry dwarfs from the deep land of Bism and brought them up near the surface of the earth to Shallowlands

---

[18]*Prince Caspian* (New York: Macmillan, 1951), pp. 41-42.
[19]Hamilton [Lewis], "Victory," *Spirits in Bondage*, p. 16.
[20]Richard Wagner, *The Ring of the Nibelung* (New York: Garden City, 1939), p. 38.

to work for her in a state of glum amnesia. She is planning a great invasion of Narnia. The idea of invasions and battles is basic to those books.

"Enemy-occupied territory — that is what this world is," Lewis plainly states in *Mere Christianity*.[21] Yet he consciously avoids slipping into dualism, which he defines as "the belief that there are two equal and independent powers at the back of everything, one of them good and the other bad, and that this universe is the battlefield in which they fight out an endless War" (p. 33).

In *The Last Battle* the form of the evil power is roughly the shape of a man, but it has the head of a bird of prey with a cruel, curved beak and long bird-like claws. It carries a deathly smell.[22] This creature closely resembles the old Priest of Ungit in *Till We Have Faces,* who looks like a dreadful vulture and bears the evil Ungit smell with him.[23]

"If evil has the same kind of reality as good, the same autonomy and completeness, our allegiance to good becomes the arbitrarily chosen loyalty of a partisan."[24] Lewis makes it clear in *The Lion, the Witch and the Wardrobe* that the power of evil is inferior to the power

[21]New York: Macmillan, 1952, p. 36.
[22]London: The Bodley Head, 1956, pp. 85-86.
[23]Grand Rapids, Michigan: Eerdmans, 1966, p. 54.
[24]"Evil and God," *Spectator,* CLXVI (February 7, 1941), 141.

of good. The power of good is that of the great King:

> "He's the King. He's the Lord of the whole wood, but not often here, you understand. Never in my time or my father's time. But the word has reached us that he has come back. He is in Narnia at this moment. He'll settle the White Queen all right. . . ."
>
> "She won't turn him into stone too?" said Edmund.
>
> ". . . Turn *him* into stone? If she can stand on her two feet and look him in the face it'll be the most she can do and more than I expect of her" (pp. 63-64).

The return of spring in this book is one of the many reflections of Norse mythology in the Narnian series. This source was one of the strongest influences upon Lewis's early years. In his long poem *Dymer* he writes:

> And from the distant corner of day's birth
> He heard clear trumpets blowing and bells ring,
> A noise of great good coming into earth
> And such a music as the dumb would sing
> If Balder had led back the blameless spring
> With victory, with the voice of charging spears,
> And in white lands long-lost Saturnian years.[25]

So it is that the return of summer brings inexpressible joy to Narnia, and, the wintry witch

[25]Clive Hamilton [C. S. Lewis], *Dymer* (New York: E. P. Dutton, 1926), p. 105.

having been defeated, "Summer is queen/ Summer is queen in all the happy land."[26]

Later on, the King himself explains to the children that "though the Witch knew the Deep Magic, there is a magic deeper still which she did not know." Her knowledge went back "only to the dawn of Time."[27]

The limitations of evil are discussed in *Mere Christianity,* where Lewis states, as he does in *The Screwtape Letters,* that wickedness is the pursuit of something good in the wrong way. One can be good for the sake of goodness even when it hurts, but one cannot be bad for the sake of badness. One is cruel for the pleasure or usefulness of it, not for the sake of cruelty itself. Badness cannot be bad in the way that goodness is good, for badness is only spoiled goodness (p. 35).

Spoiled goodness is illustrated in the beginning of sin in Narnia, as related in *The Magician's Nephew.* Digory had been sent to a distant garden to fetch a silver apple. On the gate was written this verse:

Come in by the gold gates or not at all,
Take of my fruit for others or forbear.
For those who steal or those who climb my wall

---

[26]Lewis, "The Ocean Strand," *Spirits in Bondage,* p. 46.

[27]Lewis, *The Lion, the Witch and the Wardrobe,* p. 132.

Shall find their heart's desire and find despair.
(p. 141)

Digory was just turning to go back to the gates when he stopped for one last look and received a terrible shock. There stood the Witch, throwing away the core of an apple which she had eaten. The juice had made a horrid dark stain around her mouth. Digory guessed that she must have climbed in over the wall. He began to see the truth in the last line of the verse, because "the Witch looked stronger and prouder than ever . . . but her face was deadly white, white as salt" (pp. 141-44).

The King explained the result of this act to the children later. The Witch had fled from the garden to the North of the World, where she was growing stronger in dark Magic. She would not dare to return to Narnia so long as the tree was flourishing there, because its fragrance had become a horror to her. "That is what happens to those who pluck and eat fruits at the wrong time and in the wrong way," the King concluded. "The fruit is good, but they loathe it ever after" (p. 157).

The preponderance of dark magic and witches in Lewis's books gives the impression that he is greatly concerned with demonology. However, the overall tone of his work echoes the glad assurance of St. Paul, "For I am sure that neither death, nor life, nor angels, nor principalities, nor things present, nor things to come, nor powers, nor height, nor depth, nor anything else in all creation will be able to separate us from the love of God in Christ Jesus our Lord" (Romans 8:38).

In contrast to the everlasting quality of God's love, which is his principal message, Lewis reminds us that the physical world is in a process of disintegration. He seems to agree with the concept of Sir James Jeans, that "If the inanimate universe moves in the direction we suppose, biological evolution moves like a sailor who runs up the rigging in a sinking ship."[28]

In Lewis's opinion, the modern conception of progress, as popularly imagined, is simply a delusion, supported by no evidence. Darwinism gives no support to the belief that natural selection, working upon chance variations, has a general tendency to produce improvement. Lewis asserts that there is no general law of progress in biological history. He calls the idea of the world slowly ripening to perfection a myth, not a generalization from experience. He feels that this myth distracts us from our real duties and our real interests.[29]

This attitude is illustrated by the depress-

---

[28]Sayers, *The Mind of the Maker,* p. 139.

[29]"The World's Last Night," *His,* XV (May, 1955), p. 4. Also available in *The World's Last Night and Other Essays* (New York: Harcourt, Brace, 1960), pp. 93-113.

ing picture of a dying world given in *The Magician's Nephew:*

> The wind that blew in their faces was cold, yet somehow stale. They were looking from a high terrace and there was a great landscape spread out below them. Low down and near the horizon hung a great, red sun, far bigger than our sun. Digory felt at once that it was also older than ours; a sun near the end of its life, weary of looking down upon that world. To the left of the sun, and higher up, there was a single star, big and bright. Those were the only two things to be seen in the dark sky; they made a dismal group. And on the earth, in every direction, as far as the eye could reach, there spread a vast city in which there was no living thing to be seen. And all the temples, towers, palaces, pyramids, and bridges cast long, disastrous-looking shadows in the light of that withered sun. Once a great river had flowed through the city, but the water had long since vanished, and it was now only a wide ditch of grey dust.
>
> "Look well on that which no eyes will ever see again," said the Queen. "Such was Charn, that great city, the city of the King of Kings, the wonder of the world, perhaps of all worlds" (pp. 52-53).

At "The End of This Story and the Beginning of all the Others," in the Wood between the Worlds (Chapter XV, *The Magician's Nephew*), the children learned the fate of

Charn and received a warning. They saw a little hollow in the grass, with a warm, dry bottom. Aslan told them that the hollow had been the pool that they had jumped into to go to the dying world of Charn. "There is no pool now. The world is ended, as if it had never been. Let the race of Adam and Eve take warning" (p. 159).

In *The Last Battle* Jill declares, *"Our* world is going to have an end some day. Perhaps this one won't . . . wouldn't it be lovely if Narnia just went on and on . . . ?"

"Nay," she was answered, "all worlds draw to an end; except Aslan's own country." Jill was just replying that she hoped that the end of Narnia was millions of years away, when news came that Narnia was overthrown, with this message from the lips of a dying friend: ". . . remember that all worlds draw to an end and that noble death is a treasure which no one is too poor to buy."[30]

The destruction of Narnia began with the invasion of commerce and the plunder of nature by greedy men. The idyllic forest was ruthlessly destroyed in a sacrilegious turmoil by crowds of imported workers, before the rightful owners realized what was happening. This is an exact parallel to the development of the near-fatal

---

[30]*The Last Battle* (New York: Macmillan, 1956), pp. 92-95.

dangers in Lewis's adult book about Britain, *That Hideous Strength.*[31]

The actual end of Narnia was a dramatic pageant of mythical splendour. It concluded with the moon being sucked into the sun, and the world freezing forever in total darkness. Here Lewis follows the tradition of the North rather than the conventional Christian concept of destruction by fire. Peter, High King of Narnia, was given the key to the door of heaven, and locked out the cold.[32]

Lewis's response to nature, then, is threefold. First is romantic appreciation and idealization. Second is analysis leading to an acceptance of the supernatural and to speculation about it. Third is moral awareness of the force of evil in nature and of the temporal quality of our world. Each of these responses is basic to Lewis's Christian philosophy and is an important influence upon his books for children. Nature is more than a background setting for the action of his characters. "Either there is significance in the whole process of things as well as in human activity, or there is no significance in human activity itself."[33]

---

[31]*Ibid.,* pp. 26-27.

[32]*The Last Battle,* p. 159.

[33]C. S. Lewis, *The Personal Heresy* (London: Oxford, 1939), p. 29.

Chapter Three

The Coming of the Lion: Lewis's Concept of God

"They say Aslan is on the move — perhaps has already landed."

And now a very curious thing happened. None of the children knew who Aslan was any more than you do; but the moment the Beaver had spoken these words everyone felt quite different. Perhaps it has sometimes happened to you in a dream that someone says something which you don't understand but in the dream it feels as if it had some enormous meaning—either a terrifying one which turns the whole dream into a nightmare or else a lovely meaning too lovely to put into words, which makes the dream so beautiful that you remember it all your life and are always wishing you could get into that dream again. It was like that now. At the name of Aslan each one of the children felt something jump in his inside.[1]

---

[1]Lewis, *The Lion, the Witch and the Wardrobe,* p. 54.

This passage is the first reference to Aslan in the Narnia Chronicles. Through the use of this character, who sprang into the story unbidden, Lewis has expressed with disarming simplicity his many-faceted concept of God. This is the same general concept of God that St. Augustine attempted to describe without the aid of allegory:

> What art Thou then, my God? . . . Most highest, most good, most potent, most omnipotent; most merciful, yet most just; most hidden, yet most present; most beautiful, yet most strong; stable, yet incomprehensible; unchangeable, yet all-changing; never new, never old; all-renewing, and bringing age upon the proud, and they know it not; ever working, ever at rest; still gathering, yet nothing lacking; supporting, filling, and overspreading; creating, nourishing, and maturing; seeking, yet having all things. Thou lovest, without passion; are jealous, without anxiety; repentest, yet grievest not; are angry, yet serene; changest Thy works, Thy purpose unchanged; receivest again what Thou findest, yet didst never lose; never in need, yet rejoicing in gains; never covetous, yet exacting usury. Thou receivest over and above, that Thou mayest owe; and who hath aught that is not Thine?[2]

As Dorothy Sayers has emphasized in *The*

[2]*The Confessions* I.iv.

Mind of the Maker, we seek to interpret the nature of God by means of analogies drawn from our own experience. One of our favorite analogies is that of a king. We talk of God's kingdom, His laws, and His dominion (p. 24). Aslan is a king — yet one must remember that he is not a king in this world, but in an animal land.

— God's Bodily Form —

"Aslan a man!" declares one of his subjects. "Certainly not. I tell you he is the King of the wood and the son of the great Emperor-Beyond-the-Sea. Don't you know who is King of Beasts? Aslan is a lion — *the* Lion, the great Lion."[3]

The use of a lion as a symbol of power is a Scriptural device. The book of Proverbs refers to "the lion, which is mightiest among beasts and does not turn back before any" (30:30, RSV). Earlier it compares the growling of a lion to the wrath of a king (20:2). The prophet Hosea goes one step further and likens the roaring of a lion to the wrath of God Himself (Hosea 11:10). Finally, in Revelation the lion is used as a specific symbol of Christ. St. John records, "Then one of the elders said to me, 'Weep not; lo, the Lion of the tribe of Judah,

---

[3]*The Lion, the Witch and the Wardrobe,* p. 54.

the Root of David, has conquered . . .'"
(5:5, RSV).

But Lewis, though clearly influenced by the Bible, does not rely upon Scriptural justification for his imagery. The nature of Narnia demands it. Dorothy Sayers, in a capricious bit of speculation, has captured the gist of this necessity:

> There is, of course, no reason why an infinite Mind should not reveal itself in an infinite number of forms, each being subject to the nature of that particular form. It was said, sneeringly, by someone that if a clam could conceive of God, it would conceive of Him in the shape of a great, big clam. Naturally. And if God has revealed Himself to clams, it could be only under conditions of perfect clamhood, since any other manifestation would be wholly irrelevant to clam nature. By incarnation, the creator says in effect: "See! this is what my eternal Idea looks like in terms of my own creation; this is my manhood, this is my clamhood, this is my characterhood in a volume of created characters."[4]

The scene in which the children first meet the eternal Idea in *The Lion, the Witch and the Wardrobe* is one of awe. They don't know what to do or say when they see him. People who have not been in Narnia think sometimes that a thing cannot be good and terrible at the same time. If the children in this story had ever

[4]*The Mind of the Maker*, p. 90.

thought so, they were cured of it now. When they tried to look at Aslan's face, they just caught a glimpse of the golden mane and the great, royal, solemn, overwhelming eyes; and then they found that they couldn't look at him at all and "went all trembly" (p. 103).

In contrast to the faun-like God of Kenneth Grahame's *The Wind in the Willows*,[5] a book which Lewis enjoyed,[6] the God in Lewis's books is not semi-animal; He is super-animal. Such a super-animal is conceived of in *The Problem of Pain:*

> But if there is a rudimentary Leonine self, to that also God can give a "body" as it pleases Him — a body no longer living by the destruction of the lamb, yet richly Leonine in the sense that it also expresses whatever energy and splendour and exulting power

---

[5]Kenneth Grahame also reveals God to children in a form suitable to the creatures in his story. In an extensive poetic passage, the enraptured Rat and Mole approach the Divine Presence. Mole raised his fearful eyes and saw the kind Friend and Helper; the graceful sweep of his horns, the hooked nose, the bearded smile, the strong arms and broad chest, the panpipes in his hand, and the shaggy limbs and hooves. "All this he saw, for one moment breathless and intense, vivid in the morning sky; and still, as he looked, he lived; and still, as he lived, he wondered" — Kenneth Grahame, *The Wind in the Willows* (New York: Scribner's, 1954), pp. 135-36.

[6]*Surprised by Joy*, p. 34.

dwelled within the visible lion on this earth. . . . I think the lion, when he has ceased to be dangerous, will still be awful: indeed, that we shall then first see that of which the present fangs and claws are a clumsy, and satanically perverted, imitation. There will still be something like the shaking of a golden mane. . . .[7]

Lewis's description of Aslan seems to be based on the great archetypical lion in *The Place of the Lion,* by Lewis's friend Charles Williams:

> . . . the shape of a full grown and tremendous lion, its head flung back, its mouth open, its body quivering. It ceased to roar, and gathered itself back into itself. It was a lion such as the young men had never seen in any zoo or menagerie; it was gigantic and seemed to their dazed senses to be growing larger every moment. Of their presence it appeared unconscious; awful and solitary it stood, and did not at first so much as turn its head. Then, majestically, it moved; it took up the slow forward pacing in the direction which the man had been following; it passed onward, and while they stared it entered into the dark shade of the trees and was hidden from sight.[8]

The same impregnable, awesome stateliness was encountered by the first human beings to

[7]New York: Macmillan, 1948, pp. 130-31.
[8]Grand Rapids, Michigan: Eerdmans, 1972, pp. 14-15.

accidentally see Aslan at the beginning of
Narnia in *The Magician's Nephew*. In read-
ing this passage, one notes the similarity to
Williams' account:

> It was coming on, always singing, with a slow,
> heavy pace. . . . Though its soft pads made no
> noise, you could feel the earth shake beneath
> their weight. . . . The children could not
> move. They were not even quite sure that
> they wanted to. The Lion paid no attention
> to them. Its huge red mouth was open, but
> open in song not in a snarl. It passed by them
> so close that they could have touched its
> mane. They were terribly afraid it would
> turn and look at them, yet in some queer way
> they wished it would. But for all the notice
> it took of them they might just as well have
> been invisible and unsmellable. When it had
> passed them and gone a few paces further it
> turned, passed them again, and continued its
> march eastward (pp. 95-96).

Aslan possesses the same twofold nature that
Lewis, in his theological writings, attributes to
Christ. It is the paradox of orthodox Christianity: Jesus was fully human and at the same
time fully divine. Lewis's commentary on this
doctrine is an elaboration on the principle that
everywhere the great enters the little. Its power
to do so is almost the test of its greatness. Because he believes in the power of the Higher,
just in so far as it is truly Higher, to come down,

[54]

the power of the greater to include the less,[9] Lewis presents a God capable of becoming a true lion.

His thinking on this point developed in accordance with the teaching of G. K. Chesterton. As Chesterton expressed the principle:

> The more we know of higher things the more palpable and incarnate we shall find them. . . . Not till we know the high things shall we know how lowly they are. . . . Meanwhile, the modern superior transcendentalist will find the facts of eternity incredible because they are so solid; he will not recognize heaven because it is so like the earth.[10]

The true beasthood of Aslan is made clear in *The Horse and His Boy*. The horse Bree is smugly stating his sophisticated concept of Aslan's form to his friends. With alarm they watch an enormous lion, bigger and more yellow and beautiful and alarming than any other, approaching him from behind. Bree is just explaining that when people spoke of him as a Lion they meant only that he was as strong as a lion or as fierce as a lion. It would be absurd to suppose that he was a *real* lion. It would be disrespectful. If he was a lion he would have to be a Beast just like everyone else. . . .

In revealing himself, Aslan urges the now

[9]*Miracles*, pp. 134-35.
[10]*William Blake*, p. 210.

frightened horse to test his bodily form: "Do not dare not to dare. Touch me. Smell me. Here are my paws, here is my tail, these are my whiskers. I am a true Beast."[11] In the Gospel of John, Christ said to Thomas, "Put your finger here, and see my hands; and put out your hand, and place it in my side; do not be faithless, but believing" (20:27, RSV).

Although God manifests Himself in Narnia in the form of a real lion, there is a chameleon-like inconsistency in the size and appearance of this lion. In *The Horse and His Boy* Aslan appears to be no more than a large cat when he comforts a lonely little boy named Shasta, who is hiding among the tombs at night (p. 71). In a different situation in the same book, Aslan runs so swiftly that two runaway children think there are two fierce lions chasing them on opposite sides of the road. Thus he forces them together despite their mutual distrust (p. 24). Again, Aslan appears to Shasta shining like the morning sun and taller than his horse (pp. 139-40).

In the other books there are similar variations in Aslan's revelations of himself. The first time Jill sees him in *The Silver Chair* he is lying with his head raised and his two forepaws out in front, like the lions in Trafalgar

---

[11]*The Horse and His Boy* (New York: Macmillan, 1954), pp. 169-70.

Square (p. 16). When he comes to her at the conclusion of the story, he has become so bright and real and strong that everything else begins at once to look pale and shadowy in comparison (p. 202). In *The Magician's Nephew* Digory returns from a difficult assignment and finds Aslan bigger and more beautiful and more brightly golden and more terrible than he had thought him before (p. 119).

In *Prince Caspian* Aslan himself gives part of the explanation for his changeability. Lucy had just been reunited with him after a long separation:

> "Aslan," said Lucy, "You're bigger."
>
> "That is because you are older, little one," answered he.
>
> "Not because you are?"
>
> "I am not. But every year you grow, you will find me bigger." (p. 117)

Lewis seems to believe that the more spiritually mature a person becomes, the greater capacity he will have for comprehending the grandeur and goodness of God. In his book *The Great Divorce,* souls must even develop the ability to enjoy the grandeur and goodness of heaven.[12]

The great Lion has not been divested of godly omnipotence in his animal form, any more than he has lost his grandeur or goodness.

---

[12]New York: Macmillan, 1946, pp. 55-56.

Of course he makes it clear that he, too, conforms to basic laws. In one conversation he asks Lucy reproachfully, "Do you think I wouldn't obey my own rules?"[13] One must remember, however, that in Lewis's concept of nature there can be supernatural rules which subordinate ordinary rules.

Aslan could leap with a single bound over high castle walls; the blast of his roaring would bend the trees like grass in a breeze, and the stream of his breath could blow a person thousands of miles through the air. He is powerful —yet he is all tenderness. In *Prince Caspian* he roared, "And now, where is this little Dwarf . . . who doesn't believe in lions?" and pounced upon the Dwarf, picking him up in his mouth like a mother-cat does to a kitten, and shaking him till his armor rattled. Then he tossed him up in the air and caught him gently in his huge velveted paws and set him back on the ground. He asked the breathless Dwarf, no longer cynical, to be his friend (pp. 128-29).

In *The Lion, the Witch and the Wardrobe* Lucy and Susan, already his friends, are privileged to a whole romp with Aslan. When it is over, they are no longer tired or hungry or thirsty. Lucy could never decide whether it was more like playing with a thunderstorm or playing with a kitten (p. 133).

---

[13]*The Voyage of the "Dawn Treader,"* p. 132.

Although Aslan occasionally granted such familiarity to his special followers, his awesome majesty was never diminished. Their feelings toward him could best be summarized by a portion of the dialogue from *The Wind in the Willows:* "Afraid?" murmured the Rat, his eyes shining with unutterable love. "Afraid! Of *Him?* O, never, never! And yet — and yet — O, Mole, I am afraid!" (p. 136).

This reverential dread is not unwarranted in Lewis's constructions. His own concept of the nature of Christ is more severe than the popular concept of today. Lewis contradicts what he terms the common idea that Christ preached a simple and kindly religion which was corrupted into something cruel and complicated by St. Paul. He proposes that in fact all the most terrifying texts are from the lips of the Lord, and that those which are more indicative of the salvation of all men have come from St. Paul.[14]

So it is that Aslan is a stern as well as a loving and kind personality. When in *The Lion, the Witch and the Wardrobe* the Beavers are trying to explain Aslan to the children, the girls are frightened to learn that he is not a man, but a lion. One of them ventures that she would feel rather nervous about meeting a lion. The Beaver answers that such was to be expected,

---

[14]"Introduction" to J. B. Phillips, *Letters to the Young Churches: A Translation of the New Testament Epistles* (New York: Macmillan, 1948), p. ix.

because if anyone could appear before Aslan without his knees knocking, he must be unusually brave or else just silly. The girl asks if he was, then, unsafe. Mr. Beaver replies, "Who said anything about safe? 'Course he isn't safe. But he's good. He's the King, I tell you" (p. 64).

— God's Authority —

The attempt to reconcile Christianity with other religions is attacked by Lewis in *The Last Battle* when the Narnians are told that the kingship of Aslan did not discount Tash, pagan god of the Calormenes: "Tash is only another name for Aslan. All that old idea of us being right and the Calormenes wrong is silly. We know better now. The Calormenes use different words but we all mean the same thing." Tash and Aslan were only two different names for "you know Who," and there could never be any quarrel between them. Tash was Aslan, Aslan was Tash. Aslan meant no more than Tash (pp. 37-39).

When King Tirian tries to ask how the terrible god Tash who fed on the blood of his people could possibly be the same as the good Lion by whose blood all Narnia was saved, he is attacked by soldiers and taken away. Soon everyone is taught to speak of "Tashlan." The dreadful results of this deception culminate in the eventual appearance of Tash, a type of the eschatological Antichrist figure mentioned in the letters of John. Aslan gives over the Tash worshippers to the monster they had promoted. "Thou shalt have no other gods before me" (Exodus 20:3).

⁴Aslan displayed his uncompromising, fearfully demanding nature when Jill first met him in *The Silver Chair*. He was displeased with her for her behavior to her companion. Now she was alone and very thirsty. She found a stream, but the great strange lion stood between her and the water. With a heavy, golden voice he bade her come and drink if she was thirsty. Finally she admitted to him that she was nearly frantic with thirst. Again he bade her drink. Awkwardly, she asked him to go away while she drank, but his only answer was a look and a very low growl.

> "Will you promise not to — do anything to me, if I do come?" said Jill.
> "I make no promise," said the Lion. . . .
> "Do you eat girls?" she asked.
> "I have swallowed up girls and boys, women and men, kings and emperors, cities and realms," said the Lion. It didn't say this as if it were boasting, nor as if it were sorry, nor as if it were angry. It just said it.
> "I daren't come and drink," said Jill.
> "Then you will die of thirst," said the Lion.
> "Oh dear!" said Jill, coming another step nearer. "I suppose I must go and look for another stream then."

[61]

"There is no other stream," said the Lion.
(p. 17)

Of course Jill's thirst overcame her reluctance and was immediately quenched by the amazingly cold and refreshing water. It cleared her thinking so that she yielded to the Lion and stood before him to admit that she had done wrong. Then he told her the purpose for which he had called her out of her own world. Jill objected to this idea, explaining that she had not been called. She had called out and asked for a way of escape, then found an open door which let her into this other land. "You would not have called to me unless I had been calling to you," said the Lion (p. 19).

The Calvinistic idea of God seeking out his own followers rather than the followers seeking God on their own initiative is basic to Lewis's thought. Lewis agrees with Newman that we are not merely imperfect creatures who must be improved: we are rebels who must lay down our arms.[15] As followers of the greatly contrasting "Quaker tradition of Christian mysticism"[16] have expressed this proposition, religion is God's concern, not ours. He is the Aggressor, the Invader, the Initiator. He is urgently, actively breaking into time and working through

---

[15]*The Problem of Pain* (New York: Macmillan, 1948), p. 79.

[16]Walsh, *C. S. Lewis, Apostle to Skeptics*, p. 171.

those who allow Him to lay hold upon them.[17]

In "The Shoddy Lands" God is not allowed to lay hold upon the woman whose mind is being explored. A patient knocking can be heard by the visitor, and with the knocking comes a voice which turns his bones to water: "Child, child, child, let me in before the night comes."[18]

Aslan's pursuit of those he loves recalls Francis Thompson's unrelenting Hound of Heaven:

Fear wist not to evade as Love wist to pursue.
    Still with unhurrying chase,
    And unperturbèd pace,
Deliberate speed, majestic instancy,
    Came on the following Feet,
    And a Voice above their beat —
"Naught shelters thee, who wilt not shelter Me."

. . . .

    Now of that long pursuit
    Comes on at hand the bruit;
That Voice is round me like a bursting sea:
    "And is thy earth so marred,
    Shattered in shard on shard?
Lo, all things fly thee, for thou fliest Me!"

. . . .

    Halts by me that footfall:
    Is my gloom, after all,

---

[17]Thomas R. Kelly, *A Testament of Devotion* (New York: Harper, 1941), pp. 97-99.
[18]*The Best from Fantasy and Science Fiction: Sixth Series*, p. 165.

Shade of His hand, outstretched caressingly?
   "Ah, fondest, blindest, weakest,
   I am He Whom thou seekest!
Thou dravest love from thee, who dravest Me."[19]

Shasta is brought face to face with this pursuit in *The Horse and His Boy*. He was riding a sluggish horse aimlessly along a narrow mountain road in the middle of the night. The mists were so thick that he did not know he was winding along the edge of a precipice. He had no idea where the road would take him. Gradually he became aware of a large presence pacing along between him and the gorge. He could not make his horse break into a gallop to escape, so finally he whispered, "Who are you?" The creature answered, "One who has waited long for you to speak." The Thing breathed warmly on his hands and face to assure him that it was not something dead. Then he told it of his many misfortunes, and of all the lions that had chased him on his adventures (pp. 136-38).

"There was only one lion," the Voice declared. "I was the lion" (p. 138). After recounting his part in Shasta's adventures, the Voice answered Shasta's bewildered question, "Who *are* you?"

> "Myself," said the Voice, very deep and low so that the earth shook: and again "Myself,"

[19]*The Hound of Heaven* (Mount Vernon, New York: Peter Pauper), pp. 6, 20, 22-23.

loud and clear and gay: and then the third time "Myself," whispered so softly you could hardly hear it, and yet it seemed to come from all round you as if the leaves rustled with it. (p. 139)

"I AM THAT I AM," God had answered to that question asked by Moses in the Old Testament (Exodus 3:14).

Then the morning came, and when Shasta glanced at the Lion's face he slipped out of the saddle and fell at its feet. The strange and solemn perfume of its mane was all round him, as the High King above all kings stooped and touched his forehead with its tongue. Then in a swirl of brightness the Lion disappeared, and all that was left was a deep paw print in the grass. It brimmed full of water, and soon a little stream was running down the hill (pp. 140-41).

Shasta refreshed himself in the same extremely cold, clear water that Jill's thirst had driven her to taste under such different circumstances at the beginning of *The Silver Chair*. This seems to be the same water that issued from the white rock of protection during the last battle in Narnia. It was so delicious that while the doomed children were drinking they were perfectly happy and could think of nothing else.[20] Aslan deals with each individual in a unique way to bring him to the same place. But

[20]Lewis, *The Last Battle*. p. 131.

he does not give an account of his relationship with any one person to any other person. When asked, he always answers, "I am telling you your story, not hers. I tell no-one any story but his own."[21] As Christ said when asked, "What about this man?", ". . . what is that to you? Follow me!" (John 21:22, RSV).

The most unique individual approach to Aslan is that of Emeth, a Calorman who claimed that he would gladly die a thousand deaths if he might look once on the face of Tash. He passed through the fatal door to the hovel in which Tash was supposedly dwelling, and found himself in a fair land which he thought might be the country of Tash. But as he sought Tash he met Aslan, and fell at his feet expecting death. At the sight of Aslan he realized that he had been mistaken in serving Tash all of his days. Nevertheless, he felt that it was better to see the Lion and die than to be emperor of the world and not have seen him.

— God's Love —

When Aslan welcomed him, Emeth confessed that he was no son of his, but the servant of Tash. Aslan answered, "Child, all the service thou hast done to Tash, I account as service done to me." When the truth constrained Emeth to say that he had been seeking

[21]*The Horse and His Boy,* pp. 140-41.

Tash all his days, Aslan assured him that unless his desire had been for Aslan, he would not have sought so long and so truly — "For all find what they truly seek."[22] Christ had said, "Seek and ye shall find" (Matthew 7:7).

After his conversion Emeth declared, "...my happiness is so great that it even weakens me like a wound. And this is the marvel of marvels, that he called me Beloved. . . ."[23] Unknown to him at the time of his conversion, he had already passed into the afterlife by passing through the door.

In every story there is found the same indescribable, almost ecstatic, joy and beauty at the climax when one has really met Aslan. It is the answer to that desire expressed so longingly by St. Augustine in *The Confessions:* "Oh! that I might repose on Thee! Oh! that Thou wouldest enter into my heart, and inebriate it, that I may forget my ills, and embrace Thee, my sole good!" (I. v): The bitterness of Swinburne's lines "Thou hast conquered, O pale Galilean, / The world has grown grey from Thy breath" is completely contradicted by the rich golden joy exhaled by Aslan.

Lewis writes that the man who has passed through the experience of catastrophic conversion feels like one who has waked from night-

---

[22]*The Last Battle*, p. 166.
[23]*Ibid.*, p. 167.

mare into ecstasy. Like an accepted lover, he feels that he has done nothing, and never could do anything, to deserve such astonishing happiness. Buoyant humility results.[24]

Before writing his children's books, Lewis had attested:

> The deception is . . . in that prosaic moralism which confines goodness to the region of Law and Duty, which never lets us feel in our face the sweet air blowing from 'the land of righteousness,' never reveals that elusive Form which if once seen must inevitably be desired with all but sensuous desire — the thing (in Sappho's phrase) 'more gold than gold.'[25]

Aslan was solid and real and warm, and there was lion-strength magic in his mane. When Lucy buried her face in it she became brave. It was beautiful, rich, and shining. Ever since the girls first saw him, they longed to bury their hands in the sea of fur and stroke it. The wonderful qualities of Aslan's mane and his embrace and his warm breath remind one of the ecstatic peace which the princess always found in the arms of her fairy grandmother with long golden hair in George MacDonald's *The Princess and the Goblin*.

As the Quaker mystic Thomas Kelly has expressed this personal experience with God, `

---

[24]*English Literature in the Sixteenth Century*, p. 33.
[25]*George MacDonald*, pp. 21-22.

One emerges from such soul-shaking, Love-invaded times into more normal states of consciousness. But one knows ever after that the Eternal Lover of the world, the Hound of Heaven, is utterly, utterly real, and that life must henceforth be forever determined by that Real. Like Saint Augustine one asks not for greater certainty of God but only for more steadfastness in Him.[26]

The power of the physical manifestations of Aslan's love is clearly shown in the passage in *The Magician's Nephew* in which Digory desperately dared to entreat Aslan for some cure for his dying mother back in our world. In despair he looked up at Aslan's face, and was shocked at what he saw:

> For the tawny face was bent down near his own and (wonder of wonders) great shining tears stood in the Lion's eyes. They were such big, bright tears compared with Digory's own that for a moment he felt as if the Lion must really be sorrier about his Mother than he was himself. "My son, my son," said Aslan. "I know. Grief is great. Only you and I in this land know that yet. Let us be good to one another." (p. 127)

After Aslan told Digory what he must do to rectify the troubles of Narnia, he drew a deep breath, leaned down, and gave him a lion's

---

[26] *A Testament of Devotion*, p. 57.

kiss. And Digory felt new strength and courage at once, unmindful of the fact that Aslan had made him no promises about his mother.

C. S. Lewis constantly preaches that love is something more stern and splendid than mere kindness. As he explains in *The Problem of Pain,* "Kindness, merely as such, cares not whether its object becomes good or bad, provided only that it escapes suffering." Speaking of the love of God, he asserts that if God is love, He is by definition something more than mere kindness. It appears that though God has often rebuked us and condemned us, He has never regarded us with contempt. He has paid us the intolerable compliment of loving us in the deepest, most tragic, most inexorable sense (p. 29).

The question of ungodly persons does not arise within the original Christian experience. When men try to build a system, says Lewis, very troublesome problems and very dark solutions appear.[27]

— God's Justice and Mercy —

The love of Aslan for his creation causes him to grant it justice. In *Prince Caspian* the sound of his faraway roar awakens the slumbering soldiers in the camp of the evil king, and they stare palely in one another's faces and grasp

[27]*English Literature in the Sixteenth Century,* p. 33.

their weapons. They can sense that vengeance is coming (pp. 129-30). In this book the end of the evil people is simple defeat in battle. In some of the other books, however, the fate of rebels is of more complex spiritual significance.

Uncle Andrew, for example, the foolishly wicked magician of *The Magician's Nephew,* refused to hear anything except growlings and roarings when Aslan spoke. Aslan was unable to teach him the folly of his thinking or to comfort him in the distress he brought upon himself.

This kind of situation is decried in *The Great Divorce:*

> Good beats upon the damned incessantly as sound waves beat on the ears of the deaf, but they cannot receive it. Their fists are clenched, their teeth are clenched, their eyes fast shut. First they will not, in the end they cannot, open their hands for gifts, or their mouths for food, or their eyes to see. (p. 127)

"Oh Adam's sons, how cleverly you defend yourselves against all that might do you good!" Aslan exclaimed.[28] He then gave the silly old man the only gift the man was still able to receive in his terrified state, that of sleep and temporary peace. After his harrowing adventures in Narnia, Andrew finally learned his lesson and never again tried magic when he was

---

[28]*The Magician's Nephew,* p. 153.

returned to his own world. But he was still a vain, foolish old man.

In *The Last Battle* a group of Dwarfs exasperatingly refused to accept any of the good things that were offered to them because of their obsession against being "taken in." The Dwarfs are for the Dwarfs, they would stubbornly repeat. Aslan gave them up to themselves at last, explaining that they had chosen cunning instead of belief. "Their prison is only in their own minds, yet they are in that prison; and so afraid of being taken in that they cannot be taken out. But come, children. I have other work to do" (p. 150).

The villain of *The Horse and His Boy* is even more cruel and proud than Uncle Andrew and comes to a more ignominious end. This selfish Prince Rabadash is given every chance to repent and receive mercy at the hands of the good kings he had wronged. All that Aslan asked him to do was to forget his pride, for he had nothing to be proud of, and his anger, for no one had done him wrong. In answer, Rabadash grimaced and shrieked. He called Aslan a demon and cursed all of Narnia with fiery eloquence. His tirade was ended only as, after repeated warnings from Aslan, he turned into a ridiculous donkey (pp. 185-87).

🌣 But even this punishment is tempered with mercy. Rabadash would at an appointed time resume his original shape, though he would always be restricted to a ten-mile radius around the temple in his city. Therefore he could no longer go to war, and was always the laughing-stock of his country. Lewis's philosophy of dealing with sin is that of Thomas More: "The devil . . . the prowde spirite . . . cannot endure to be mocked."[29]

Aslan used physical affliction in a more serious manner to effect the cure of sin as well as the punishment of sin. In *The Voyage of the "Dawn Treader"* Eustace is turned into a dragon because of his irresponsibility, childishness, and selfishness. In the form of this ugly beast he learns to value his friends and to help others. Tolkien says that the dragon "has the trade-mark *Of Faerie* written plain upon him." As a boy, he "desired dragons with a profound desire. . . . The world that contained even the imagination of Fafnir was richer and more beautiful, at whatever cost of peril."[30] The peril for Eustace is that of being left alone on the island, stranded by his size.

One night a huge lion came to him. He shut his eyes tight, but the lion told him to follow, and he could not disobey. They went to a mountain garden with a well in the center. There were marble steps going down into it,

[29]As quoted in C. S. Lewis, *The Screwtape Letters* (New York: Macmillan, 1943), p. [7].

[30]"On Fairy Stories," p. 63.

and Eustace was sure that the clear water would ease the pain in his leg. But the lion told him that he must undress first.

Eustace realized that this must mean for him to shed his dragon skin, and he found that it came off easily. But as he entered the pool again, he saw that he was covered with another skin like the first one. Three times he peeled off his dragon skin, only to find another one underneath. Then the lion told him that he must let the lion undress him. Eustace was afraid of the claws, but he submitted. The lion tore deep, and the pain was excruciating, but when it was over, Eustace was clean. The water smarted at first, but then it felt delicious, and he realized that he had become a boy again. But he was a new boy.[31]

Lewis believes that acknowledging one's sinful condition and being willing to be delivered from any carnal determent to spiritual well-being are essential to conversion. In his imaginative book *The Great Divorce,* Lewis tells about a ghost who had a little red lizard riding on his shoulder and whispering in his ear. A flaming angel offered to relieve him of the little monster, but he was reluctant to have it killed for fear of being hurt himself. As the angel approached, the ghost cried out in distrust because he was being burned. The angel

---

[31]*The Voyage of the "Dawn Treader,"* pp. 88-91.

explained, "I never said it wouldn't hurt you. I said it wouldn't kill you" (p. 101). When the distraught ghost finally submitted, he was delivered from the reptile and transformed into a radiant young man.

The inability of Eustace and of the ghost to cleanse themselves is true of all men and illustrates the doctrine in Lewis's chapter in *Mere Christianity* entitled "Nice People or New Men." Nasty people, if they make any attempt at goodness at all, learn more quickly than naturally good people that they need help. "It is Christ or nothing for them" (p. 166).

The sin of traitorous Edmund in *The Lion, the Witch and the Wardrobe* was paid for more dearly than that of Eustace. Edmund had joined the forces of the White Witch and was saved by the followers of Aslan just as she was about to murder him in return for his services. The next morning Aslan and Edmund went walking together, and when they returned Edmund was a different person. What Aslan had said to him, no one else ever knew (p. 112).

But soon the witch appeared, claiming the traitor as her lawful prey. The magic which the Emperor had put into Narnia at the beginning decreed that for every treachery she would have a right to kill. She renounced her claim on Edmund's blood only when Aslan offered himself as substitute (pp. 114-15). As Lewis explains in the Psyche myth of *Till We Have*

Faces, "In the Great Offering the victim must be perfect" (p. 56).

Aslan's atonement for Edmund's sin took place at the great Stone Table that very night. He surrendered himself to a howling and gibbering crowd of evil spirits and monsters, who bound him tightly and sheared away his luxurious mane. Then they jeered and mocked him and put a muzzle on his face. Throughout his torment he never moved.[32]

Such a scene is described by Lewis in *Dymer:*

That moment in a cloud among the trees
Wild music and the glare of torches came.
On sweated faces, on the prancing knees
Of shaggy satyrs fell the smoky flame,
On ape and goat and crawlers without name,
On rolling breast, black eyes and tossing hair,
On old bald-headed witches, lean and bare.

They beat the devilish tom-tom rub-a-dub;
Lunging, leaping, in unwieldy romp,
Singing Cotytto and Beelzebub,
With devil dancers mask and phallic pomp,
Torn raw with briars and caked from many a
        swamp
They came, among the wild flowers dripping blood
And churning the green mosses into mud. (p. 82)

After the diabolical crowd had its fill of expressing its frenzy by kicking and spitting upon

---

[32]*The Lion, the Witch and the Wardrobe,* p. 125.

the lion, they hoisted him onto the Stone Table. There the witch told him gloatingly that his sacrifice was in vain because next she would kill Edmund. Then she plunged a great stone knife into his lion heart.[33]

While the two girls kept vigil over his body during the night, hundreds of little mice came and nibbled away his bonds. Then, as the girls watched the sun rise they heard a great noise from the direction of the Table. They turned and saw that it had been rent from one end to the other into two pieces. The body was gone. Just as they expressed their grief, Aslan spoke to them from behind. He had been resurrected, his rich golden mane restored (p. 134).

Tolkien says that

> It is the mark of a good fairy-story, of the higher or more complete kind, that however wild its events, however fantastic or terrible the adventures, it can give to child or man that hears it, when the 'turn' comes, a catch of the breath, a beat and lifting of the heart, near to (or indeed accompanied by) tears, as keen as that given by any form of literary art, and having a peculiar quality.[34]

The "turn" of this fairy story is the resurrection of Aslan:

> You can say that Christ died for our sins.

---

[33]*Ibid.*, p. 126.

[34]"On Fairy Stories," p. 81.

You may say that the Father has forgiven us because Christ has done for us what we ought to have done. You may say that we are washed in the blood of the Lamb. You may say that Christ has defeated death. They are all true. If any of them do not appeal to you, leave it alone and get on with the formula that does. And, whatever you do, do not start quarrelling with other people because they use a different formula from yours.[35]

The point that Lewis insists upon is that mere time can never wash out the guilt. That can be done only by repentance and the blood of Christ. Even this, however, cannot cancel the *fact* of a sin, because all times are eternally present to God. Therefore, if we repent of our sins we should remember the price of our forgiveness and remain humble.[36] Edmund's memory of his own past mistakes made it easier for him to be patient and eager to forgive others from that time on.

Although the Gospels culminate in these two phases of Christ's activities, His death and resurrection, the epistles of St. Paul tell us that He was also the Creator:

For by him were all things created, that are in heaven, and that are in earth, visible and invisible, whether they be thrones, or domin-

---

[35]Lewis, *Mere Christianity,* pp. 141-42.
[36]*The Problem of Pain,* p. 49.

ions, or principalities, or powers: all things
were created by him, and for him.

(Colossians 1:16)

— God's Creativity and Care —

The genesis of Narnia occurs in *The Magician's Nephew*. When the children and their
strange companions accidentally arrived at
Narnia, it was Nothing. They found themselves
in an expanse of cold dry darkness. At last a
voice began to sing far away, the most beautiful
noise they had ever heard. Then the sky burst
full of stars, all singing in cold, tingling, silvery
voices which joined the First Voice. As the
children watched, the Voice sang a whole world
into existence, part by part, and color by color.
When they saw the Singer, it was a Lion
(pp. 87-90).

After the Lion had created a host of animals
from the ground, he went to and fro among
them, occasionally selecting a pair and touching their noses with his own. When all of the
chosen ones had gathered around him, Aslan
stared hard at them, and they all changed. The
small ones grew larger, a few of the great ones
grew smaller, and many stood up on their hind
legs. Then he breathed out a long warm
breath,[37] there was a flash like fire,[38] and the

---

[37]Cf. Genesis 2:7.
[38]Cf. Acts 2:3.

deepest, wildest voice they had ever heard said, "Narnia, Narnia, Narnia, awake. Love. Think. Speak. Be divine waters" (p. 103). All of the magical woods people came forth. "Creatures, I give you yourselves," continued Aslan in his strong, happy voice. "I give to you forever this land of Narnia. I give you the woods, the fruits, the rivers. I give you the stars and I give you myself" (p. 105).

By this creative power, and his consequent death and resurrection, Aslan almost completely fills the description of Christ in the first chapter of Hebrews:

> God . . . hath in these last days spoken unto us by his Son, whom he hath appointed heir of all things, by whom also he made the worlds; Who being the brightness of his glory, and the express image of his person, and upholding all things by the word of his power, when he had by himself purged our sins, sat down on the right hand of the Majesty on high. . . . (1:1-3)

But after Aslan's resurrection, he did not simply retire to the side of the Emperor Beyond the Sea. "He'll be coming and going," the children were told. "One day you'll see him and another you won't. He doesn't like being tied down — and of course he has other countries to attend to. It's quite all right. He'll often drop in. Only you mustn't press him. He's wild, you know. Not like a *tame* lion."[39] When Aslan dropped in this way, it was usually to instruct, guide, or correct his subjects.

Aslan employed "eye-for-an-eye, tooth-for-a-tooth" punishment for purposes of instruction when he appeared one time to Aravis in *The Horse and His Boy*. When she ran away from home, she had cast her stepmother's slave into a drugged sleep, for which the young girl was beaten. Aslan tore Aravis's back with his claws so that her scratches were equal to the stripes on the slave's back. He explained to her later that she needed to know what it felt like, and she understood (p. 171).

Sometimes just the sight of Aslan was enough to make the children aware of their mistakes and guide them in their adventures. In *The Silver Chair* Jill had been distracted from her mission by greedy ambition and had forgotten the set of clues that Aslan had so carefully taught her. He appeared to her one night in a dream, full of sweetness, and although she didn't know what it was that troubled her, she began to weep. Then, to her horror, he asked her to repeat the forgotten signs. He took her to the window and she saw in the moonlight the directions she had failed to follow (p. 98).

When Jill's assignment was finally completed, Aslan returned to her to bring her home.

---

[39]*The Lion, the Witch and the Wardrobe*, p. 149.

She wanted to tell him how sorry she was for all of her mistakes, but she could not speak. Drawing her close, he touched her pale face with his tongue and said, "Think of that no more. I will not always be scolding . . ." (p. 202). It is clear that although Lewis has incorporated in Aslan the stringent discipline of the Old Testament Jehovah, he has also attributed to him the Old Testament promise: "For I will not contend for ever, nor will I always be angry . . ." (Isaiah 57:16, RSV).

The God of the Bible was the guardian and guide of His people in their physical afflictions as well as their spiritual wanderings. One of the times when Aslan appeared in such a way was at the Dark Island in *The Voyage of the "Dawn Treader."* The ship was lost in a great darkness, and the men aboard were growing panicky. Lucy whispered a plea to Aslan. Soon a whirring light appeared in the air; it was an albatross. It led them out into the light, and before it left, Lucy heard Aslan's voice whisper courage to her and felt him breathe a delicious smell in her face (pp. 156-57).

In this book the children voyaged to the end of the world, hoping to reach Aslan's land. At last they came to the place where the earth meets the sky. They waded ashore from the Silver Sea, and found waiting for them a Lamb so white that even with their eyes as strong as eagle eyes they could hardly look at it. There

were fish there roasting on a fire for their breakfast and, as in the Gospel story, the Lamb said,
"Come and have breakfast" (John 21:12).
After the most delicious food they had ever
tasted, Lucy asked the Lamb if this was the
way to Aslan's country.

The Lamb answered that for these children
the door into Aslan's country was from their
own world:

> "There is a way into my country from all the
> worlds," said the Lamb; but as he spoke his
> snowy white flushed into tawny gold and his
> size changed and he was Aslan himself, tower-
> ing above them and scattering light from his
> mane. (p. 209)

He promised that he would be telling them all
the time how to get into his country. He would
not tell them how long or short the way would
be — only that it would lie across a river. Yet
he is the great Bridge Builder.

> "But there I have another name. You must
> learn to know me by that name. This was the
> very reason why you were brought to Narnia,
> that by knowing me here for a little, you may
> know me better there." (p. 209)

The implication is that when the children
returned to their own world they would carry
with them concepts which would help them to
understand Christ. First would be the recognition of His kingship and an acceptance of the

doctrine of Incarnation. They would easily realize that incarnation does not divest Christ of His omnipotence and awesomeness. As Queen Lucy says after the Last Battle, "In our world too, a Stable once had something inside it that was bigger than our whole world."[40] His fusion of sternness and gentleness would be comprehensible because of their past experiences with Aslan. Christ would be acknowledged as the initiator of love, and surrender to His love would be known as true joy. The multiple nature of Christ would seem natural. His function as creator, judge, redeemer, instructor, and provider would all be related as aspects of the expression of God's love for mankind.

---

[40]*The Last Battle*, p. 143.

Chapter Four

Possible Gods and Goddesses: Lewis's Concept of Man

"There was once a little princess who —"
"But, Mr. Author, why do you always write about princesses?"
"Because every little girl is a princess."
"You will make them vain if you tell them that."
"Not if they understand what I mean."
"Then what do you mean?"
"What do you mean by a princess?"
"The daughter of a king."
"Very well, then every little girl is a princess. . . ."[1]

This passage from George MacDonald's *The Princess and the Goblin* serves not only as the beginning of a fairy tale, but as the starting point of C. S. Lewis's concept of man. All of Lewis's teachings about human life are based

---

[1]MacDonald, *The Princess and the Goblin*, p. 1.

upon this fundamental spiritual reverence for individuals. Lewis feels that next to the Blessed Sacraments one's neighbor is the holiest object presented to the senses.

In his book *The Weight of Glory,* Lewis says that the glory of one's neighbor is so heavy that only humility can carry it — it will break the backs of the proud. It should be laid on each of us daily. This weight is the realization that we live in a society of possible gods and goddesses. He explains that even the dullest and most uninteresting person may some day be a creature which you would be tempted to worship if you saw it now, or else a horror and a corruption such as is seen only in a nightmare. He concludes, "All day long we are, in some degree, helping each other to one or other of these destinations."[2] Lewis's symbolical books are designed to help people toward what he considers the right destination.

— Human Behavior —

According to critics of modern poetry, myths define the relationship of man to himself and to God in such a way that there is no distinction between symbol and meaning. A distinction grows, however, as the civilization declines. Before the separation is complete, mythologies may be used by laymen and artists to describe

---

[2]Grand Rapids, Michigan: Eerdmans, 1965, pp. 14-15.

man's place in the universe. "In this sense, a mythology may serve as a guide, explaining conduct and regulating ethics on both material and spiritual planes."[3] Lewis's series of children's books fill this capacity. The structure of all of their mythical plots is the problem of human behavior.

The philosophy behind Lewis's presentation of human problems in an unfamiliar point in space and time is not, as might be supposed, what Lewis calls the idea of the Unchanging Human Heart.[4] In *The Pilgrim's Regress* Lewis attacks that method satirically by letting his shameless Mr. Sensible advocate the idea that people are always the same although dress and manners vary like shifting disguises.[5] In *A Preface to Paradise Lost* Lewis suggests a more valuable approach to literature: "Instead of stripping the knight of his armour you can try to put his armour on yourself . . ." (p. 62). This is the approach which his books naturally evoke from the reader. He seeks to show the reader how it would feel to have the honor, wit, royalism, and gallantries of the characters depicted.

The medieval ideal of chivalry and knight-

---

[3]Kimon Friar and John Malcolm Brinnin, *Modern Poetry* (New York: Appleton-Century-Crofts, 1951), pp. 421-22.
[4]*A Preface to Paradise Lost*, p. 61.
[5]Grand Rapids, Michigan: Eerdmans, 1958, p. 86.

hood is venerated throughout Lewis's writing. Lewis believes that this old tradition is practical and vital. It taught the great warrior humility and forbearance, and it demanded valor of the urbane and modest man. Lewis feels that if we cannot produce brave yet gentle Lancelots we will produce men who are either brutal in peace or cowardly in war. Then the world will be divided between wolves who cannot understand and sheep who cannot defend the things which make life desirable.[6]

The first evidence of knightly behavior in the Narnia Chronicles occurs when the boy Peter saves his sister's life by attacking a monstrous wolf with his sword and slaying it. "Peter did not feel very brave; indeed, he felt he was going to be sick. But that made no difference to what he had to do."[7] Afterwards, Aslan surprises him by causing him to kneel, striking him with the flat of the blade, and titling him Sir Peter Fenris-Bane. When the children have conquered the rest of their adversaries in this adventure, they are crowned the four rulers of Narnia and reign in chivalric fashion for many happy years.

In this system they gradually grow and change, like the man in a story Lewis tells in

---

[6]"Importance of an Ideal," *Living Age*, CCCLIX (October, 1940), 110-11.

[7]*The Lion, the Witch and the Wardrobe*, p. 106.

Mere Christianity. For many years this man had to wear a mask that made him look much more handsome than he really was. When he finally took it off, he discovered that his own face had grown to fit it and that he was truly beautiful (p. 146). Similarly, young Peter becomes King Peter the Magnificent, a tall, deep-chested warrior. Susan comes to be Queen Susan the Gentle, a gracious and beautiful woman. Edmund is called King Edmund the Just, because he is great in council and judgment. And little Lucy becomes Queen Lucy the Valiant, the most gay and spirited of all. By following Aslan's will for them, they live together in great joy and richness.

In all of Lewis's stories for children, the will of God proves to be the source of ultimate delight. Throughout *The Pilgrim's Regress,* a book for adults, John seeks the delightful Islands of the West in vain. Only when he ventures the long, difficult journey to the righteous Mountains of the East does he realize that the Mountains of the East are, in fact, the Islands of the West.

In accordance with this theory, obedience is the key to happiness. Aslan uses varying methods to reveal his will to the children in Narnia. In *The Silver Chair* he explains the task he has set before them and charges them to seek to fulfill it until they had done so, or died in the attempt, or else gone back into their own world. He gives them four signs to guide them on their quest and warns them to repeat the signs over and over every day, letting nothing turn their minds from following them (p. 19).

Aslan gave these directions on his holy mountain. He warned them that the air would thicken as they dropped down to Narnia, and they must be careful not to become confused. The signs would not look at all as they would expect them to look; so it was important for them to remember them and pay no attention to appearances. Aslan had spoken clearly to them on the mountain, but he would not often do so down in Narnia.

At other times Aslan did not explain to the children in advance what he wanted them to do. He chose to reveal himself to them and guide them at his own discretion. In *Prince Caspian* the children are journeying through the wilds of Narnia in an attempt to reach the prince in time to save him from destruction. They had made the wrong turn. Suddenly Lucy, who loved Aslan the most, saw him for a moment in the other direction. The other children didn't quite believe her, especially when she said that Aslan wanted them to go the other way:

> "How do you know that was what he wanted?" asked Edmund.
> "He — I — I just know," said Lucy, "by his face." (p. 104)

Despite Lucy's tears, they journeyed on in the wrong direction. Later, when they had realized their mistake, Aslan came to guide them back in the right direction through the night. Lucy was still the only one who could see him and be sure of his presence for a long time. Edmund had more faith than the other two, and eventually he saw the lion shadow, then Aslan himself moving on ahead. It was harder for Peter, who had been very stubborn. Susan was the last of the four to see the great figure, and she was greatly ashamed. It had not been true doubt that had hidden Aslan from her, but fears. This passage demonstrates that sins of attitude can separate man from God (pp. 125-26).

When Lucy encountered Aslan alone, she began to criticize the others for not believing her when she had first seen him. She heard the faintest suggestion of a growl coming from somewhere deep inside him. She apologized.

> ". . . But it wasn't my fault anyway, was it?" The Lion looked straight into her eyes.
> "Oh, Aslan," said Lucy. "You don't mean it was? How could I — I couldn't have left the others and come up to you alone, how could I? Don't look at me like that . . . oh well, I suppose I *could*. Yes, and it wouldn't have been alone, I know, not if I was with you. . . ." (pp. 117-18)

Whenever the children had committed any

sin by their actions or their thoughts, a look or a word from Aslan was sufficient as a reprimand. It was only in his presence, however, that they fully realized the danger or the seriousness of their shortcomings. They were good children, as judged by common standards, but they fell far short of the total goodness which Aslan's nature seemed to seek for them.

— Sin and Evil —

This is the situation experienced by a Christian. According to J. B. Phillips, the Christian aspires to a level of life which he is not spiritually robust enough to maintain. "He can see that it is right, and he can desire, even passionately, to follow the new way, but in actual practice he does not achieve this new quality of living."[8]

C. S. Lewis believes that the great sin is the sin of pride or self-conceit. It was through pride that the devil became the devil, the complete anti-God state of mind. Pride leads to every other vice. It gets no pleasure out of having something, only out of having more of it than the next man. Most of the evils which people attribute to greed or selfishness are the result of pride. In *Mere Christianity,* Lewis observes

---

[8]*Your God Is Too Small* (New York: Macmillan, 1955), p. 132.

that pride is not something that God forbids us because of concern for His own dignity. He simply wants to eliminate this barrier between Himself and His creation (pp. 94-99).

Because Lewis believes the sin of pride to be the primary force of evil in our own world, it is to be expected that pride is the initial form of evil in his children's books. The introduction of sin into Narnia is in the person of Jadis, the proud, cruel queen of the dead world of Charn. This witch gloried in the power she had once wielded over the greatest city of all worlds, and set out to conquer new worlds so that she would have more subjects to honor and obey her. She hated Aslan and did not see him as he really was.

In God, according to *Mere Christianity,* one encounters something which in every respect is immeasurably superior to oneself. As long as one is proud, one cannot know God. "As long as you are looking down, you cannot see something that is above you" (p. 96). This is why Jadis did not recognize Aslan to be the rightful king of Narnia.

Lewis points out that the more pride one has, the more one dislikes pride in others. Jadis exemplified this behavior when she blamed the destruction of Charn upon her sister. "At any moment I was ready to make peace —" she said, "yes, and to spare her life too, if only she would yield me the throne. But she would not.

Her pride has destroyed the whole world."[9] Jadis was incapable of realizing that it was her own pride that had caused the tragedy.

This dazzlingly beautiful queen believed that her subjects belonged to her like cattle. Her overweening sense of superiority led her to exempt herself from the common rules of ethics and morality. As she loftily explained this principle to the children, ". . . what would be wrong for you or for any of the common people is not wrong in a great Queen such as I. The weight of the world is on our shoulders. We must be freed from all rules. Ours is a high and lonely destiny."[10]

These same words were spoken by the foolish magician in *The Magician's Nephew,* who ranked himself with all profound students and great thinkers and sages, "men like me who possess hidden wisdom" (p. 16). When Digory saw through his uncle's other grand words, he realized that all they meant was that he thought he could do anything he wanted.

Pride is also a common failing of the children. When it occurs, it always keeps them from full fellowship with Aslan. Accordingly, Aslan commended every display of humbleness. Every time he gave someone a commission of honor and responsibility, it was with the attitude that

[9]*The Magician's Nephew,* p. 53.
[10]*Ibid.,* p. 55.

he expressed in *Prince Caspian* by saying, "If you had felt yourself sufficient, it would have been a proof that you were not" (p. 173).

In *The Lion, the Witch and the Wardrobe,* it was pride that caused Edmund to deny his experience in Narnia to his brother and sister who had never been there. Afterwards, when all four of them were there together, he decided that the others were not paying enough attention to him. This was his imagination; but the witch's promise that she would make him a prince was tempting him, so he sneaked away and betrayed the others to her. He had been duped by her flattery.

The other reason Edmund betrayed his true friends was the vice of greed. The witch had fed him enchanted Turkish delight, which would make the eater desire more and more, even enough to kill him. This food had the opposite effect of Lewis's refreshing Perelandrian science-fiction fruit, which was too delicious to eat for mere self-indulgence. One would not gorge himself on that fruit for fear of vulgarity.[11] But Edmund had become oblivious to vulgarity. He couldn't even enjoy any food that he ate later, because there is nothing that ruins the taste of good ordinary food so much as the memory of bad magic food.[12]

---

[11]*Perelandra* (New York: Macmillan, 1952), pp. 38-39.
[12]*The Lion, the Witch and the Wardrobe,* p. 71.

This is only one of the times when the evil enchantment of greed is employed in an attempt to cause the children to sin against Aslan. It also distracted the children from the signs they were following in *The Silver Chair,* when the lovely Lady in green beguiled them with promises of warmth and rich food and ease at the castle of the giants (p. 74). In *The Voyage of the "Dawn Treader"* the children had landed on the island Death-water. There they discovered a pool that turned any object immersed in it to solid gold. Within minutes they were under its curse and began to fight among themselves. Only the distant appearance of Aslan broke the spell and gave them a chance to escape with their old natures intact (pp. 105-06).

Whether the element involved is gold or luxury or food or feminine beauty, enchantments are always brought on by evil disguised as innocent attractiveness. In *The Lion, the Witch and the Wardrobe,* Edmund's encounter with the witch (p. 24), which led to his enchantment, is parallel to the story of little Kay meeting the evil snow queen in "The Snow Queen" by Hans Andersen. Both of these witches appear in great sledges, dressed in white fur. Both are tall and beautiful and seem almost perfect to the eyes of their little victims; but both are as cold and pale as white ice. As soon as the boys are enchanted, they are no longer afraid. They feel very important, try to show off, and indiscreetly tell anything that is asked of them.

The vague uneasiness experienced in this state is concisely expressed by Andersen when Kay tells the queen that he could do mental arithmetic as far as fractions and knew the number of square miles and the number of inhabitants in the country. The queen always smiled, and then it seemed that what he knew was not enough. . . .[13] This same uncertainty is attributed to Mark Studdock in Lewis's novel *That Hideous Strength*, after he joins the league of evil called the N. I. C. E. He is greedy for the things this diabolical organization offers to him, but after he confusedly accepts the terms presented, he feels more inadequate and uneasy than before.

Greed is the first tool of enchantment. The other one, perhaps more important, is the technique of mental confusion and the subjugation of intelligence by emotional persuasion and fallacious rationalization. This is illustrated by the first temptation, that of the apple in the garden in *The Magician's Nephew*. Digory knew that he was forbidden to take the apple of life for any use of his own. He had been told to carry it to Aslan. But as he was leaving,

---

[13]Hans Christian Andersen, *Fairy Tales* (New York: Garden City Publishing Company, 1932), p. 142.

the witch confronted him and told him that if he didn't stop to listen to her he would miss some knowledge that would make him happy all his life. Although Digory knew better, he listened (p. 144).

He withstood the temptation to eat of the fruit himself, but when the witch tried to persuade him that if he really loved his mother he would steal the fruit to heal her, he weakened. She contrasted his rightful devotion to his mother with his thoughtless obedience to a wild animal in a strange world that was none of his business. She made him feel muddled and guilty, but he insisted that he was bound by his promise to the lion, whether it was right or not. Speaking ever-so-sweetly, the witch rationalized away his promise, but made one fatal mistake. She suggested that he could use his magic ring to return to his own world with the apple and leave his friend Polly behind. This meanness made the rest of the witch's reasoning sound false, and suddenly Digory's head cleared (pp. 146-47).

A stronger enchantment is worked and more painfully overcome in *The Silver Chair*. The beautiful witch hides her anger and throws green powder in the fireplace, filling the room with a very sweet and drowsy smell. Then she begins a steady, monotonous thrumming on the strings of her instrument. It becomes very difficult to think. She speaks sweetly and quietly, with a kind, soft, musical laugh. She tells the children, the prince, and Puddleglum that the world above the ground that they spoke of is all a dream. Although they rouse themselves several times and try to argue with her, it is easier to succumb, and a relief to admit that she is right:

> Then came the Witch's voice, cooing softly like the voice of a wood-pigeon from the high elms in an old garden at three o'clock in the middle of a sleepy, summer afternoon. . . .
>
> "You have seen lamps, and so you imagined a bigger and better lamp and called it the *sun*. You've seen cats, and now you want a bigger and better cat, and it's called a *lion*. Well, 'tis a pretty make-believe, though, to say truth, it would suit you all better if you were younger. And look how you can put nothing into your make-believe without copying it from the real world, this world of mine, which is the only world." (pp. 151-53)

The trick of lulling the victim's reasoning powers to sleep is advocated by Screwtape in his letters to Wormwood. "By the very act of arguing," says Screwtape, "you awake the patient's reason; and once it is awake, who can foresee the result?" The business of the tempter is to fix his victim's attention upon the stream of immediate sense experiences. "Teach him to call it 'real life' and don't let him ask what he means by 'real'."[14] The devils fear to let humans think about the realities they can't touch and see. The goal of Satan is befuddlement.

"There is nothing like a good shock of pain for dissolving certain kinds of magic," Lewis observes when the spell of the witch is broken.[15] Puddleglum, in one last desperate attempt against the wiles of the witch, stamped the fire with his bare feet. The pain cleared his head, the smell cleared the heads of the others, and the disruption infuriated the witch.

Her magic undone, the witch reverted to her hideous serpent form. This transformation is similar to one that occurs in *The Place of the Lion* by Charles Williams (pp. 170-71). Her arms merged into her sides, and her legs were intertwined with each other as she became a writhing pillar of poison green. All of her face disappeared except the elongated nose and flaming eyes, browless and lashless. The prince slew this thick serpent as it coiled its loathsome body around him for the kill. Lewis teaches that the enchantment of evil can be overcome, but that it demands strength, self-sacrifice, and clear thinking. Evil is a paradox of beauty and horror, and destroys men by deceiving them.

Aslan has no patience with people who blame enchantments for their failures. In *The Magi-*

---

[14]Lewis, *The Screwtape Letters*, p. 12.
[15]Lewis, *The Silver Chair*, p. 154.

cian's Nephew Digory had struck a magic bell, despite the warning below it, because he was curious. He had told his friend Polly, "I expect anyone who's come as far as this is bound to go on wondering till it sends him dotty. That's the Magic of it, you see. I can feel it beginning to work on me already" (p. 45). Then he fought with her when she tried to constrain him. When he gives an account of his actions to Aslan, he adds that he thinks he must have been a bit enchanted by the writing under the bell.

> "Do you?" asked Aslan; still speaking very low and deep.
> "No," said Digory, "I see now I wasn't. I was only pretending." (p. 121)

Unprincipled curiosity, the Faustian lust for knowledge, causes many of the troubles in this series. It is Uncle Andrew's insatiable greed for wisdom, not tempered with any sense of moral responsibility, that leads to the original invasion of Narnia by the evil Queen Jadis. Lewis refers to the motivation of magicians in his *English Literature in the Sixteenth Century,* the third volume in *The Oxford History of English Literature:*

> . . . We see at once that Bacon and the magicians have the closest possible affinity. Both seek knowledge for the sake of power (in Bacon's words as 'a spouse for fruit' not a 'curtesan for pleasure'), both move in a

[101]

grandiose dream of days when Man shall have been raised to the performance of 'all things possible.' (p. 13)

Queen Jadis herself, in *The Magician's Nephew,* is the paramount example of this perversion, causing the destruction of the world of Charn by acquiring knowledge that she is not meant to wield. It is the secret of the Deplorable Word. She tells the children proudly:

> "It had long been known to the great kings of our race that there was a word which, if spoken with the proper ceremonies, would destroy all living things except the one who spoke it. But the ancient kings were weak and soft-hearted and bound themselves and all who should come after them with great oaths never even to seek after the knowledge of that word. But I learned it in a secret place and paid a terrible price to learn it." (p. 54)

Whatever price Jadis paid, the price paid by the rest of her race is higher. Aslan told the children when they returned to their own world that the race of Adam and Eve must take warning from this example.

> "But we're not quite as bad as that world, are we, Aslan?"
> "Not yet, Daughter of Eve," he said. "Not yet. But you are growing more like it. It is not certain that some wicked one of your race will not find out a secret as evil as the

> Deplorable Word and use it to destroy all
> living things. . . ." (p. 160)

The insinuation here about weapons of international warfare is the most specific symbolic commentary upon a social problem in current affairs to be found in Lewis's books for children.

Many other problems of individual behavior are handled in these books. These include vanity, spying, theft, frivolity, quarreling, prudishness, and bullying. Their imaginative treatment embodies the traditional Christian attitude toward such sins, but presents it in a lively narrative manner.

One of these problems is stressed more than any of the others. It is the problem of cowardice. Cowardice, Lewis contends, is the only vice which is purely painful. Men have become proud of most vices, but not of this one. Hatred has its pleasures, so it is often the compensation by which a man reimburses himself for his fear and shame.[16]

"Perfect love, we know, casteth out fear. But so do several other things—ignorance, alcohol, passion, presumption and stupidity."[17] Courage is the only acceptable answer to fear, and it is chief of the virtues. Lewis agrees with Johnson that where courage is not, no other virtue can

---

[16]*The Screwtape Letters,* p. 147.

[17]Lewis, "The World's Last Night," p. 23.

survive except by accident.[18] "A chastity or honesty, or mercy, which yields to danger will be chaste or honest or merciful only on conditions. Pilate was merciful till it became risky."[19]

— Heroism and Hierarchy —

The most courageous character in Narnia is a large talking mouse named Reepicheep. He exemplifies knightly valor to the point of fool-hardiness, but Aslan favors him for this fear-lessness. He is introduced in *Prince Caspian* as a gay and martial mouse with a tiny rapier at his side and long whiskers which he twirls like a moustache. His speech of allegiance to the prince is given with the flair, made ludicrous by his small size, which characterizes his every speech and action: " 'There are twelve of us, Sire,' he said with a dashing and graceful bow, 'and I place all the resources of my people un-reservedly at your Majesty's disposal' " (p. 65).

Reepicheep is at the fore of every battle, but the culmination of his career is his journey to the utter East, to the land of Aslan. His life's ambition is to venture to the end of the world and never return. In *The Voyage of the "Dawn Treader"* he fulfills this daring ambition. His attitude toward adventure is summarized in his challenging answer to the question of what use

---

[18]*Surprised by Joy*, p. 153.
[19]*The Screwtape Letters*, pp. 148-49.

it would be to sail into the mysterious blackness of the Dark Island:

> If by use you mean filling our bellies or our purses, I confess it will be no use at all. So far as I know we did not set sail to look for things useful but to seek honour and adventures. And here is as great an adventure as ever I heard of, and here, if we turn back, no little impeachment of all our honours. (p. 150)

The antithesis of this attitude is expressed in *The Pilgrim's Regress* by Mr. Sensible. He advocates moderation in all things, claiming that the secret of happiness lies in knowing where to stop. Travel should serve to quiet, without satiating, a liberal curiosity and to provide interesting memories. But when it comes to crossing a canyon, a modest tour along one side is sufficient and much less dangerous (p. 100). Thus, with irony, Lewis has expressed for adults the lesson which Reepicheep expresses more directly.

It is Reepicheep who partakes of the food and drink offered to the travellers at an enchanted table to prove its safety. When they had asked the girl there how they could know that she was a friend, she had answered, "You can't know. . . . You can only believe — or not."[20] Reepicheep always dares to believe. He finds answers by direct experience.

---

[20]*The Voyage of the "Dawn Treader,"* p. 169.

When at last he leaves the others to go on alone, he knows that he will need his sword no longer; so he casts it into the lilied sea, where it stands upright with its hilt above the surface. This Arthurian symbolism ratifies him as the ideal of Christian valor. As he bids his friends good-bye he tries to be sad for their sakes, but he is trembling with happiness.

Thirty-three years before the publication of *The Voyage of the "Dawn Treader,"* Lewis published a poem titled "Our Daily Bread," which includes these stanzas anticipating the story of Reepicheep:

Often me too the Living voices call
In many a vulgar and habitual place,
I catch a sight of lands beyond the wall,
    I see a strange god's face.

And some day this will work upon me so
I shall arise and leave both friends and home
And over many lands a pilgrim go
    Through alien woods and foam,

Seeking the last steep edges of the earth
Whence I may leap into the gulf of light
Wherein, before my narrowing Self had birth,
    Part of me lived aright.[21]

The ultimate reward of courage, or of love (which, as the virtue which casts out fear, is related to courage), is justified by Lewis at the

---

[21]*Spirits in Bondage,* pp. 86-87.

beginning of *The Weight of Glory,* where he stresses the positive aspect of virtue:

> If you asked twenty good men to-day what they thought the highest of the virtues, nineteen of them would reply, Unselfishness. But if you asked almost any of the great Christians of old he would have replied, Love. You see what has happened? A negative term has been substituted for a positive, and this is of more than philological importance. The negative ideal of Unselfishness carries with it the suggestion not primarily of securing good things for others, but of going without them ourselves. I do not think this is the Christian virtue of Love. The New Testament has lots to say about self-denial, but not about self-denial as an end in itself. We are told to deny ourselves and to take up our crosses in order that we may follow Christ; and nearly every description of what we shall ultimately find if we do so contains an appeal to desire. If there lurks in most modern minds the notion that to desire our own good and earnestly to hope for the enjoyment of it is a bad thing, I submit that this notion has crept in from Kant and the Stoics and is no part of the Christian faith. (p. 1)

"Goodness, armed with power, is corrupted; and pure love without power is destroyed."[22] This statement by Reinhold Niebuhr in *Be-*

---

[22]Sayers, *The Mind of the Maker,* p. 201.

yond Tragedy expresses Lewis's attitude toward Christianity and government. Lewis openly embraces the maxim, "All power corrupts." He goes on to say, "The loftier the pretensions of the powers, the more meddlesome, inhuman, and oppressive it will be. Theocracy is the worst of all possible governments."[23] In Narnia the government is divinely ordained, but it is not a theocracy. It took the form of an oligarchy which later became a monarchy.

Lewis believes in political equality, though only because of its protective function. He distinguishes between two views of democracy. What he calls the false, romantic doctrine is the theory that all men are so good and so wise that they deserve a share in the government and the government needs their advice. Lewis holds rather that fallen men are too wicked to be trusted with any irresponsible power over each other.[24] His answer is "Let us wear equality; but let us undress every night."[25]

Corruption and bureaucracy are not tolerated in the series for children. In *The Last Battle* Shift, the ape, comes into power by telling the

[23]"Lilies That Fester," *Twentieth Century,* CLVII (April, 1955), 335. Also available in *The World's Last Night and Other Essays,* pp. 31-49, and *They Asked for a Paper,* pp. 105-19.
[24]*The Weight of Glory,* p. 77.
[25]"Equality," *Spectator,* CLXXI (August 27, 1943), 192.

naive donkey, "You know you're no good at thinking, Puzzle, so why don't you let me do your thinking for you?" (p. 12). The outcome of Puzzle's submission is the destruction of Narnia.

When Prince Caspian found a similar situation in his Lone Islands, he overthrew the governor by force, in a scene rather like that of Christ cleansing the temple.[26] The major social evil which he revoked was that of slavery. The governor insisted that the Prince didn't understand the economic problem involved. Caspian replied that he didn't see that slavery brought to the islands any food, drink, books, music, horses, or other objects worth having, and that it was to be stopped.[27] Lewis does not disagree with Aristotle's statement that some people are fit only to be slaves. But he rejects slavery because he sees no men fit to be masters:[28]

> "But that would be putting the clock back,"[29] gasped the governor. "Have you no idea of progress, of development?"
> "I have seen them both in an egg," said Caspian. "We call it *Going bad* in Narnia. . . ."[30]

---

[26]Lewis, *The Voyage of the "Dawn Treader,"* p. 45.
[27]*Ibid.*, p. 48.
[28]"Equality," p. 192.
[29]In the chapter "We Have Cause to be Uneasy" in *Mere Christianity,* Lewis points out that if the clock is wrong, putting it back is often a sensible thing to do (p. 22).
[30]*The Voyage of the "Dawn Treader,"* p. 48.

There is little reference to politics in this series of children's books, because Lewis feels that only a sick society must think much about the subject, as a sick man must think about his digestion. Digestion and politics are the means to an end, not an end in themselves. The end of the secular community is to facilitate and safeguard the family, friendship, and solitude. Lewis quotes Dr. Johnson in saying that the end of all human endeavor is to be happy at home.[31] This is the secular end of all behavior in Narnia.

Lewis glorifies the state of kings and queens and feels that they are an asset to society. He contends, "Where men are forbidden to honour a king they honour millionaires, athletes, or film stars instead: even famous prostitutes or gangsters. For spiritual nature, like bodily nature, will be served; deny it food and it will gobble poison."[32]

There was responsibility for the rulers of Narnia as well as glory, however. As the voyagers neared the end of the world, Prince Caspian decided to go on with Reepicheep instead of returning to his kingdom in Narnia. Only when Aslan personally commanded him to let the others go on and to return alone to Narnia, did Caspian tearfully realize that he

---

[31]*The Weight of Glory*, p. 32.
[32]"Equality," p. 192.

had no choice. Lewis expresses this principle in a commentary upon the works of William Morris:

> In the later romances the claims of the tribe are not forgotten, and the young hero who goes to the end of the world to drink of the well of life carries thither with him, and carries back, the determination to settle down and be a good king in his own small country. No wanderings are allowed to obliterate our love for "the little platoon we belong to."[33]

The return to Narnia in *The Voyage of the "Dawn Treader"* was not really sad for Caspian, because the beautiful girl of the enchanted table, the daughter of a star, was waiting for him to take her back with him as his bride. This is the only incident involving romantic love in the Narnian series. The prince, hoping to break the enchantment of three sleeping lords, had told the girl of the story in our world in which the prince couldn't break the enchantment until he had kissed the princess. "But here," she answered, "It is different. Here he cannot kiss the princess till he has dissolved the enchantment" (p. 170). This gentle repartee was the extent of their courtship as recorded by Lewis. The lack of emphasis upon romantic love in the

---

[33]C. S. Lewis, "William Morris," *Rehabilitations and Other Essays* (London: Oxford, 1939), p. 50. Also available in *Selected Literary Essays,* ed. Walter Hooper.

Narnia stories is intentional—they were written for children — but it is fairly typical of all of Lewis's writing. Notable exceptions are the novel *That Hideous Strength*, his personal account of the death of his wife Joy in *A Grief Observed*, and his studies of Courtly Love, the love poetry of Donne, and the role of romantic love in Christian morality.

His only commentary upon family life in the Narnia books is at the beginning of *The Voyage of the "Dawn Treader."* He describes the home environment of Eustace Clarence Scrubb, a priggish, nasty little boy who almost deserved his unhappy name. His father and mother had taught him to call them by their Christian names, which Lewis considers a perverse notion. It is, he says, an effort to ignore the difference in kind which makes for real organic unity.[34] These parents were vegetarians, nonsmokers, and teetotallers and wore a special kind of underclothes. Very little furniture graced their house, and there were few bedclothes and open windows. They did not want an ordinary son.

As a result of his progressive rearing, Eustace preferred animals dead and pinned on cards. He liked only books of information, preferably those illustrated with pictures of grain elevators or fat foreign children doing exercises in model schools (p. 1). Lewis laments this approach to

---

[34]*The Weight of Glory*, pp. 34-35.

learning: "The hours of unsponsored, uninspected, or perhaps even forbidden reading, the ramblings and 'long, long thoughts' in which those of luckier generations first discovered literature and nature and themselves, are a thing of the past."[35]

In *The Silver Chair* Lewis caustically describes Eustace's school (p. 1). It was very progressive, unruly, and corrupt. The other extreme, a dull, stiff, authoritarian girls' school in Narnia is exposed just as mercilessly in *Prince Caspian* (pp. 166-67). Lewis states his conservative attitudes on child training and education in "The World's Last Night": "For my own part I hate and distrust reactions not only in religion but in everything. Luther surely spoke very good sense when he compared humanity to a drunkard who, after falling off his horse on the right, falls off it next time on the left" (p. 2).

A subject less commonly discussed than love, family relations, and education demands more of Lewis's attention. It is the problem of the position of animals in society and their relation to man.

The use of anthropomorphic beasts is discussed by William Empson in his consideration of *Alice in Wonderland*. He says that the talking-animal convention and changes of rela-

---

[35]"Lilies That Fester," pp. 336-37.

tive size evidently make some direct appeal to the child even though more sophisticated ideas are piled into them. Ever since Aesop, talking animals have been used for didactic purposes.[36] But in Lewis's books there is a real concern for the animals themselves. Tolkien claims that talking beasts in fairy tales are founded on "the desire to converse with other living things," which is "as ancient as the Fall." He says that a vivid sense of the separation between man and beast is very ancient: but also a sense that it was a severance and that a guilt lies on us. "Other creatures are like other realms with which Man has broken off relations, and sees now only from the outside at a distance, being at war with them, or on the terms of an uneasy armistice."[37]

Lewis seems to have been influenced by the domestic nature attributed to animals by other writers. We might note, for example, the following passage from Hans Christian Andersen:

> "Will you fly out free?" asked the Princess, "or will you have fixed positions as court crows, with the right to everything that is left in the kitchen?"
> And the two Crows bowed, and begged for fixed positions, for they thought of their old

[36]William Empson, *Some Versions of Pastoral* (Norfolk, Connecticut: James Laughlin, New Directions, 1935), p. 265.
[37]"On Fairy Stories," p. 80.

age, and said, "It is so good to have some provisions for one's old days." . . .[38]

The character of these crows is like the character of the beaver couple in *The Lion, the Witch and the Wardrobe*. The beavers are tidy, provincial people of modest means who value security.

In real life Lewis did not grant animals the wealth of sacred individuality which they enjoy in his fancies. He classified man as the only amateur animal; all the others are professionals:

> They have no leisure and do not desire it. When the cow has finished eating she chews the cud; when she has finished chewing she sleeps; when she has finished sleeping she eats again. She is a machine for turning grass into calves and milk — in other words, for producing more cows . . . if they could speak they would all of them, all day, talk nothing but shop.[39]

In a letter to Lewis, Evelyn Underhill criticized such tame concepts of the animal kingdom:

> Is the cow which we have turned into a milk machine or the hen we have turned into an egg machine really nearer the mind of God than its wild ancestor? . . . Your own example of the good-man, good-wife, and good-dog in

[38]*Fairy Tales*, p. 161.
[39]*Rehabilitations*, p. 83.

the good homestead is a bit smug and utili-
tarian, don't you think, over against the wild
beauty of God's creative action in the jungle
and deep sea. . . . Of course I agree that
animals too are involved in the Fall and await
redemption and transfiguration. (Do you
remember Luther looking up from Romans
viii 21 and saying to his dog, "Thou too shalt
have a little golden tail"?) And man is no
doubt offered the chance of being the medi-
ator of that redemption. But not by taming,
surely? Rather by loving and reverencing the
creatures enough to leave them free. . . .[40]

Lewis did not disagree with her. In fact, he
incidentally expressed his sympathy with the
wildness and freedom of animals in his poem
about men "Under Sentence":

There is a wildness still in England that will
    not feed
In cages; it shrinks away from touch of the
    trainer's hand;
Easy to kill, not easy to keep. It will not breed
In a zoo for the public pleasure. It will not
    be planned.

Do not blame us too much if we, being
    woodland folk
Cannot swell the rejoicing at this new world
    you make;
We, hedge-hogged as Johnson, we unused to
    the yoke

[40]*The Letters of Evelyn Underhill,* ed. Charles
Williams (London: Longmans, Green, 1943), p. 302.

As Landor, surly as Cobbett (that badger),
    birdlike as Blake.

A new scent troubles the air — friendly to you
    perhaps —
But we with animal wisdom understand that
    smell.
To all our kind its message is guns, ferrets,
    traps,
And a ministry gassing the little holes in which
    we dwell.[41]

In the Narnian series Lewis neatly fuses these three contrasting concepts of animals (anthropomorphic domesticity, unimaginative productivity, and wildness) to effectively inculcate the doctrine of the humane treatment of animals. This is a major fact of human behavior throughout the books. Even so minor an offense as throwing stones at a stray cat is not to be winked at.[42]

In *The Horse and His Boy* a frivolous girl named Lasaraleen obnoxiously spoils her pet monkey. Yet Lewis comments upon the reaction going on at present against excessive love of pet animals. We have been taught to despise the rich, barren woman who loves her dog too

---

[41]*Spectator,* CLXXV (September 7, 1945), 219. Also published in a revised version as "The Condemned" in *Poems,* ed. Walter Hooper (New York: Harcourt, Brace, 1964), p. 63.

[42]*The Horse and His Boy,* p. 74.

much and her neighbor too little. But Lewis reminds us that one can do something for the Peke, and it can make some response. It is at least sentient.[43]

In the chapter devoted to animals in *The Problem of Pain* Lewis sums up the convictions on this subject that can be discerned in the Narnian tales. "Man was appointed by God to have dominion over the beasts, and everything a man does to an animal is either a lawful exercise, or a sacrilegious abuse, of an authority by divine right" (p. 126). As Aslan said to the first king and queen, in *The Magician's Nephew,* "You shall rule and name all these creatures, and do justice among them, and protect them from their enemies . . ." (p. 123).

— The End of Man —

To summarize, Lewis believes first in the sanctity of men and in the will of God as the first principle of human behavior in relation to God Himself, to one's fellow man, and to animals. Obedience to God's will depends upon fellowship with Him and results in chivalric behavior. Sin is inevitable, and the first sin is pride. Greed, intellectual sloth, lust for knowledge, and cowardice are the other major sins. The counterpart of the last of these, courage, is the first of the virtues. It is no secret that

---

[43]*The Personal Heresy,* p. 67.

virtue will be rewarded. Consideration for the welfare of the individual and conservatism are advocated in human relations. Although the divine right of kings would be the ideal system of human rule, in our sinful state no man should wield irresponsible power over his fellows. Man has been granted power over animals, however, and must use it wisely. These points are the key to Lewis's concept of human life on this earth. But his total concept of man is not limited to this life.

Lewis acknowledges that we cannot help wishing that human life and youth would last forever, yet he questions the wisdom of that wish. He refers to the dialectic of natural desire which William Morris hinted at when he said that life owes all its sweets to that same death whence rise all its bitters. Without the gift of death, life would become a wearisome torment.[44] An unlimited extension of life as we know it now would not be a blessing. "Neither the individual nor the community as popular thought understands them," says Lewis in *The Weight of Glory,* "can inherit eternal life: neither the natural self, nor the collective mass, but a new creature" (p. 42).

This idea is illustrated at the end of *The Silver Chair* when Old Caspian has died in Narnia. His friends, on the Mountain of Aslan,

---

[44]*Rehabilitations*, p. 51.

heard the distant, despairing funeral music and found the dead king lying on the golden gravel of a stream, with the water flowing over him and swaying his long white beard. They wept for him, and the Lion wept too. Then Aslan told the Son of Adam to pierce his paw with a great pointed thorn. A large drop of blood splashed into the stream over the body. It changed, becoming younger and younger, then leaped up before them as a young man or a boy. In Aslan's country people have no particular ages. Lewis contends that even in this world, it is the stupidest children who are most childish and the stupidest grown-ups who are most grown-up.

In *The Last Battle* the transformed bodies of the children are described. They were all cool, fresh, and clean, with splendid, yet comfortable, clothes, and faces somehow nobler than ever before. All of their physical infirmities had disappeared, along with their ages.

Although the new Caspian was strong and joyous after his resurrection, the children were apprehensive because they knew he had died. Aslan told them good-naturedly that most people have died. He had himself. Then Caspian told them that he would be a ghost if he appeared in Narnia again, but one can't be a ghost in one's own country. The best part of it was that Caspian could no longer want wrong things, and whatever he did would be right.[45]

The forces of evil could no longer affect him. Even the rebellion and eternal condemnation of the sinful witch could no longer infect his happiness. Lewis denies

> the demand of the loveless and the self-imprisoned that they should be allowed to blackmail the universe: that till they consent to be happy (on their own terms) no one else shall taste joy: that theirs should be the final power; that Hell should be able to veto Heaven.[46]

At the end of Narnia millions of creatures, all of the living men and beasts of that world, came streaming toward the doorway where Aslan waited. As they approached him, some of their faces filled with fear and hate. And these swerved to his left, disappearing into his huge black shadow. Those who loved him came in at the Door at his right.

Later, inside, Aslan turned to the children and said that they did not look so happy as he meant them to be. They answered that they were greatly afraid of being sent away, because they had been sent back into their own world so often.

---

[45]*The Silver Chair*, p. 205.
[46]*The Great Divorce*, p. 124.

[121]

"No fear of that," said Aslan. "Have you not guessed?"

Their hearts leaped and a wild hope rose within them.

"There *was* a real railway accident," said Aslan softly. "Your father and mother and all of you are — as you used to call it in the Shadowlands — dead. The term is over: the holidays have begun. The dream is ended: this is the morning."[47]

So it is that Lewis's concept of human life is climaxed in death. One of his favorite quotations from the pen of George MacDonald expresses it best:

"You have tasted of death now," said the Old Man. "Is it good?"

"It is good," said Mossy. "It is better than life."

"No," said the Old Man. "It is only more life."[48]

[47]*The Last Battle*, p. 183.
[48]*George MacDonald*, p. 104.

Chapter Five

Weaving a Spell

> Do you think I am trying to weave a spell?
> Perhaps I am; but remember your fairy tales.
> Spells are used for breaking enchantments as
> well as for inducing them. And you and I
> have need of the strongest spell that can be
> found to wake us from the evil enchantment
> of worldliness which has been laid upon us
> for nearly a hundred years.

These words from *The Weight of Glory*
(p. 5) aptly apply to Lewis's books for children.
They are counteractive to the spirit of worldli-
ness. Although these books are richly sensuous,
this characteristic is merely an expression of the
spiritual values symbolized. Lewis finds the
same element in Scriptural imagery. He believes
that "the scriptural picture of heaven is . . . just
as symbolical as the picture which our desire,
unaided, invents for itself; heaven is not really
full of jewelry any more than it is really the

beauty of nature or a fine piece of music."[1] In *The Great Divorce* Lewis adds, "The picture is a symbol: but it's truer than any philosophical theorem (or, perhaps, than any mystic's vision) that claims to go behind it" (p. 129).

— Lewis's View of His Fairy Tales —

Lewis's own definition of his books for children would perhaps be "fantasy that hovers between the allegorical and the mythopoeic."[2] He feels that myth-making may be an art, or gift, which criticism has largely ignored:

> It may even be one of the greatest arts; for it produces works which give us (at the first meeting) as much delight and (on prolonged acquaintance) as much wisdom and strength as the works of the greatest poets. . . . It goes beyond the expression of things we have already felt. It arouses in us sensations we have never had before, never anticipated having, as though we had broken out of our normal mode of consciousness and 'possessed joys not promised to our birth'. It gets under our skin, hits us at a level deeper than our thoughts or even our passions, troubles oldest certainties till all questions are reopened, and in general shocks us more fully awake than we are for most of our lives.[3]

---

[1]*The Weight of Glory*, p. 6.
[2]*George MacDonald*, p. 14.
[3]*Ibid.*, pp. 16-17.

When he wrote this paragraph Lewis was speaking not of his own mythopoeic works, but of those of George MacDonald. He proceeded to consider the problem of whether or not this art is a species of literary art. Because a particular pattern of events composes the myth, not a particular arrangement of words, Lewis assumes that any other effective means of communication would be equally legitimate.[4] Concerning stories, Lewis suggests that the internal tension between the theme and the plot constitutes its chief resemblance to life. In real life, as in a story, something must happen. Lewis says that that is the trouble: "We grasp at a state and find only a succession of events in which the state is never quite embodied. . . ."[5] In stories the plot is only a net whereby to catch the real theme. This usually is something other than a process, with no sequence in it, and much more like a state or quality such as giant-ship, otherness, or the desolation of space.[6]

Lewis feels that "the Christian will take literature a little less seriously than the cultured Pagan." The unbeliever often attaches an almost religious significance to his aesthetic experiences and has to obey his artistic conscience like a mystical amoral law. He often feels a superiority to the great mass of mankind who

[4]*Ibid.*, pp. 14-15.
[5]"On Stories," p. 105.
[6]*Ibid.*, p. 102.

turn to books for mere recreation. In contrast, the Christian "knows that the vulgar, since they include most of the poor, probably include most of his superiors." He knows "that the salvation of a single soul is more important than the production or preservation of all the epics and tragedies in the world." Therefore he does not object to tales and comedies for mere amusement and refreshment.[7]

Lewis credits the humanists with the mistakenly serious approach to literature. They could not really bring themselves to believe that the poet cared about the shepherds, lovers, warriors, voyages, and battles. They must be only a disguise for something more 'adult.' The Medieval readers had also believed in a poet's hidden wisdom, but they did not allow the hidden wisdom to obscure the fact that the text before them was 'a noble and joyous history'. Perhaps this was because they had been taught that the multiple meanings of Scripture never abrogated the literal sense. They pressed the siege, wept with the heroine, and shuddered at the monsters.[8]

"All children's books are on a strict judgement poor books," Tolkien has said. "Books written entirely for children are poor even as

---

[7]*Rehabilitations,* p. 195. Also available in *Christian Reflections,* ed. Walter Hooper (Grand Rapids, Michigan: Eerdmans, 1967), p. 10.
[8]*English Literature in the Sixteenth Century,* p. 28.

children's books."[9] Lewis would agree. He holds that

> no book is really worth reading at the age of ten which is not equally (and often far more) worth reading at the age of fifty — except, of course, books of information. The only imaginative works we ought to grow out of are those which it would have been better not to have read at all. A mature palate will probably not much care for *creme de menthe:* but it ought still to enjoy bread and butter and honey.[10]

His own books for children appeal to adults as well as children, and are enjoyable even when read for mere amusement and refreshment in their literal meaning.

According to Lewis, the fundamental difference between the Christian writer and the unbeliever in their approach to literature is that the Christian will ask of every idea and every method not "Is it mine?", but "Is it good?"[11] In the preface to *The Allegory of Love* Lewis states, ". . . I am well aware, like the philosopher, that 'if I had succeeded in owing more, I might then perhaps have gained more of a claim to be original'."[12]

[9]"On Fairy Stories," p. 59.
[10]"On Stories," p. 100.
[11]Lewis, *Rehabilitations,* p. 195. Also, *Christian Reflections,* p. 9.
[12]London: Oxford, 1936, p. [vii].

— Lewis's View of Truth —

It is true that there is little original material in Lewis's books for children. He tapped many literary sources for the fanciful frameworks of his stories. Most of the Christian convictions expressed within these frameworks are traditional Christian beliefs freshly stated. Lewis believed in the divine creation of nature and man, the subsequent corruption of both of them, and the personal love of God which redeems them.

Lewis's credo, we have seen, can be divided into three major categories: his opinions about nature, God, and mankind. These opinions establish Lewis's position in the areas of philosophy, theology, psychology, and sociology.

Lewis's concept of nature is threefold. It consists of a romantic appreciation of untamed beauty, a rational acceptance of the supernatural, and a realistic awareness of the corruption and ultimate destruction of our present system. His concept of God is that of a creator, redeemer, and sustainer who is omnipotent, omniscient, and omnipresent. This personal God of love, simultaneously an awesome king, has the power to reveal Himself to his creation by assuming an incarnate form. Lewis's concept of mankind is based upon mankind's relationship to God. Therefore it is reverential, yet critical. Man is prone to sin, and this keeps him from the full joy of fellowship with God. Man should resist the deceptions of evil and determine his behavior toward God, other men, and animals by love. The resurrected man will enjoy an eternal life of unbroken fellowship with God. These three concepts have been graphically presented in mythological form in the Narnian tales.

Lewis expressed his feeling about mythology in relation to Christianity in *The Pilgrim's Regress,* the first book he wrote after becoming a Christian. This book has never enjoyed the popularity of many of his later works, but it was the source of the ideas in most of them.[13] At the end of his adventures the pilgrim is in the caverns, and Wisdom troubled him by saying that his experiences had been only figurative, nothing other than mythology. Then another voice, noticeably like that of Aslan, spoke to him, saying:

> "Child, if you will, it *is* mythology. It is but truth, not fact: an image, not the very real. But then it is My mythology. The words of wisdom are also myth and metaphor: but since they do not know themselves for what they are, in them the hidden myth is master, where it should be servant: and it is but of man's inventing. But this is My inventing, this is the veil under which I have chosen to

---

[13]Walsh, *C. S. Lewis, Apostle to Skeptics,* p. 49.

appear even from the first until now. For this end I made your senses and for this end your imagination, that you might see my face and live." (pp. 219-20)

Further Reading

1. "Past Watchful Dragons: The Fairy Tales of C. S. Lewis," by Walter Hooper, included in *Imagination and the Spirit,* ed. Charles Huttar. Grand Rapids, Michigan: Wm. B. Eerdmans, 1971, pp. 277-339.

This 68-page essay is intended for specialists, but is delightful reading for any adult lover of Narnia. Walter Hooper provides the reader with a masterful blending of personal warmth and zestful scholarship, plus illustrations. The essay examines elements in Lewis's childhood; the Christian transformation of those elements in Lewis's life; the nature of the fairy tale and myth; the Narnia series itself, including the land, inhabitants, and institutions of Narnia; theology (Aslan); and the desire for heaven. Also included is a valuable outline of the history of Narnia.

2. "On Three Ways of Writing for Children," by C. S. Lewis, included in *Of Other Worlds,* ed. Walter Hooper. London: Geoffrey Bles, 1966, pp. 22-34.

In this 1952 essay, Lewis concentrates upon his own way of writing for children and offers his view of the role of a children's author. He also makes a spirited defense of fairy tales and the adult enjoyment of children's books. Lewis wrote this essay while he was still composing the Narnian series.

3. "Sometimes Fairy Stories May Say Best What's To Be Said," by C. S. Lewis, included in *Of Other Worlds,* pp. 35-38.

In this 1956 essay Lewis describes his "boiling" desire to write some fairy tales, his eventual idea that these stories might carry some Christian potency, and his conviction that the Narnian series is for adults as well as for children.

4. "It All Began with a Picture," by C. S. Lewis, included in *Of Other Worlds,* p. 42.

This brief piece from 1960 recounts with brevity and good humor Lewis's memory of his creation of the Narnian series.

5. "A Letter from C. S. Lewis," by James E. Higgins, *The Horn Book Magazine,* October, 1966, pp. 533-39.

The heart of this article is a brief letter Lewis sent to James E. Higgins on December 2, 1962. Lewis answers six questions about his Narnian series. (Part of this letter is found on page 307 of the *Letters of C. S. Lewis,* edited, with a memoir, by W. H. Lewis — New York: Harcourt, Brace, 1966.)

Bibliography

A. PRIMARY SOURCES

Besides the hardcover editions listed below, *The Chronicles of Narnia* have also been published in paperback by Collier, 1970.

Hamilton, Clive (pseudonym for C. S. Lewis). *Dymer*. New York: E. P. Dutton, 1926. (Available in *Narrative Poems*. London: Geoffrey Bles, 1969.)
————. *Spirits in Bondage*. London: William Heinemann, 1919.
Lewis, C. S. *The Abolition of Man*. New York: Macmillan, 1947.
————. *The Allegory of Love*. London: Oxford, 1936.
————. *Arthurian Torso*. London: Oxford, 1948.
————. "Awake My Lute," *Atlantic Monthly,* CLXXII (November, 1943), 113.
————. *Beyond Personality*. New York: Macmillan, 1945.
————. *The Case for Christianity*. New York: Macmillan, 1943.
————. *Christian Behavior*. New York: Macmillan, 1943.

————. "The Christian Hope — Its Meaning for Today," *Religion in Life,* XXI (1951), 20-32.

————. "Donne and Love Poetry in the Seventeenth Century," *Seventeenth Century Studies Presented to Sir Herbert Grierson* (by several authors). Oxford: Clarendon, 1938. (available in *Selected Literary Essays.* London: Cambridge University, 1969.)

————. *English Literature in the Sixteenth Century.* Oxford: Clarendon, 1954.

————. "Epitaph," *Spectator,* CLXXXI (July 30, 1948), 142.

————. "Equality," *Spectator,* CLXXI (August 27, 1943), 192.

————. "Evil and God," *Spectator,* CLXVI (February 7, 1941), 141.

————. George MacDonald. New York: Macmillan, 1954.

————. *The Great Divorce.* New York: Macmillan, 1946.

————. *The Horse and His Boy.* New York: Macmillan, 1965.

————. "Importance of an Ideal," *Living Age,* CCCLIX (October, 1940), 109-11.

————. "Introduction" to D. E. Harding, *The Hierarchy of Heaven and Earth.* New York: Harper, 1952.

————. "Introduction" to J. B. Phillips, *Letters to the Young Churches: A Translation of the New Testament Epistles.* New York: Macmillan, 1940. (Available in *God in the Dock.* Grand Rapids, Michigan: Wm. B. Eerdmans, 1970.)

————. *The Last Battle.* New York: Macmillan, 1970.

————. "Lilies That Fester," *Twentieth Century,* CLXVII (April, 1955), 330-41. (Available in

The World's Last Night and Other Essays. New York: Harcourt, Brace, 1960. Also in *They Asked for a Paper.* London: Geoffrey Bles, 1962.)

―――. *The Lion, the Witch and the Wardrobe.* New York: Macmillan, 1950.

―――. *The Literary Impact of the Authorized Version.* London: University of London, Athlone Press, 1950. (Available in *Selected Literary Essays.* London: Cambridge, 1969.)

―――. *The Magician's Nephew.* New York: Macmillan, 1955.

―――. *Mere Christianity.* New York: Macmillan, 1952.

―――. *Miracles.* New York: Macmillan, 1947.

―――. "On a Picture by Chirico," *Spectator,* CLXXXII (May 6, 1954), 607. (Available in *Poems.* New York: Harcourt, Brace, 1964.)

―――. *Out of the Silent Planet.* New York: Macmillan, 1943.

―――. "The Pains of Animals," *Atlantic Monthly,* CLXXXVI (August, 1950), 559-61. (Available in *God in the Dock.* Grand Rapids, Michigan: Wm. B. Eerdmans, 1970.)

―――. *Perelandra.* New York: Macmillan, 1952.

―――. *The Personal Heresy.* London: Oxford, 1939.

―――. "Preface" to B. G. Sandhurst, *How Heathen is Britain?* London: Collins, 1947.

―――. "Preface" and "On Stories," *Essays Presented to Charles Williams* (compiled by C. S. Lewis). London: Oxford, 1947. (Available in paperback edition. Grand Rapids, Michigan: Wm. B. Eerdmans, 1966).

―――. *A Preface to Paradise Lost.* London: Oxford, 1942.

―――. *The Pilgrim's Regress.* New York: Sheed

and Ward, 1944. (Available in paperback edition. Grand Rapids, Michigan: Wm. B. Eerdmans, 1958.)

————. *Prince Caspian.* New York: Macmillan, 1951.

————. "Private Bates," *Spectator,* CLXXIII (December, 1944), 496.

————. *The Problem of Pain.* New York: Macmillan, 1948.

————. "Psychoanalysis and Literary Criticism," *Essays and Studies,* XXVII (1942), 21. (Available in *Selected Literary Essays.* London: Cambridge, 1969.)

————. *Rehabilitations and Other Essays.* London: Oxford, 1939.

————. "The Salamander," *Spectator,* CLXXIV (June 8, 1945), 521. (Available in *Poems.* New York: Harcourt, Brace, 1964.)

————. *The Screwtape Letters.* New York: Macmillan, 1943.

————. "The Shoddy Lands," *The Best from Fantasy and Science Fiction. Sixth Series* (edited by Anthony Boucher). New York: Doubleday and Company, 1957. (Available in *Of Other Worlds.* London: Geoffrey Bles, 1966.)

————. *The Silver Chair.* New York: Macmillan, 1953.

————. *Surprised by Joy.* London: Geoffrey Bles, 1955.

————. *That Hideous Strength.* New York: Macmillan, 1946.

————. *Till We Have Faces.* London: Geoffrey Bles, 1956. (Available in paperback edition. Grand Rapids, Michigan: Wm. B. Eerdmans, 1966.)

————. "To G. M.," *Spectator,* CLXIX (October 9, 1942), 335.

————. "Under Sentence," *Spectator,* CLXXV (September 7, 1945), 219.

————. *The Voyage of the "Dawn Treader."* New York: Macmillan, 1952.

————. *The Weight of Glory and Other Addresses.* New York: Macmillan, 1949. (Available in paperback edition. Grand Rapids, Michigan: Wm. B. Eerdmans, 1965.)

————. "The World's Last Night," *His,* XV (May 1955), 1-4, 22-24. (Available in *The World's Last Night and Other Essays.* New York: Harcourt, Brace, 1960.)

B. SECONDARY SOURCES

Andersen, Hans Christian. *Fairy Tales.* New York: Garden City, 1932.

Anderson, George C. "C. S. Lewis: Foe of Humanism," *Christian Century,* LXIII (December 25, 1946), 1562-63.

Auden, W. H. "Red Lizards and White Stallions," *The Saturday Review of Literature,* XXIX (April 13, 1946), 22.

Augustinus, Aurelius. *The Confessions of St. Augustine.* New York: Pocket Books, 1953.

Bacon, Leonard. "The Imaginative Power of C. S. Lewis," *The Saturday Review of Literature,* XXVII (April 8, 1944), 9.

Brady, Charles A. "Introduction to Lewis," *America,* May 27, 1944, pp. 213-14; June 10, 1944, pp. 269-70.

Chesterton, G. K. *William Blake.* London: Duckworth, 1910.

Cooke, Alistair. "Mr. Anthony at Oxford," *New Republic,* CX (April 24, 1944), 578-80.

Driberg, Tom. "Lobbies of the Soul," *New Statesman,* XLIX (March 19, 1955), 393.

Empson, William. *Some Versions of Pastoral.* Norfolk, Connecticut: James Laughlin, New Directions, 1935.

Friar, Kimon, and John Malcolm Brinnin. *Modern Poetry.* New York: Appleton-Century-Crofts, 1951.

Gilbert, Alan H. "Critics of Mr. C. S. Lewis on Milton's Satan," *South Atlantic Quarterly,* XLVII (April, 1948), 216-25.

Grennan, Margaret R. "The Lewis Trilogy: A Scholar's Holiday," *Catholic World,* CLXVII (July, 1948), 337-44.

Grahame, Kenneth. *The Wind in the Willows.* New York: Scribner's, 1954.

Haldane, J. B. S. "God and Mr. C. S. Lewis," *The Rationalist Annual.* London: Watts, 1948.

Hamilton, Edith. *Mythology.* New York: The New American Library of World Literature, 1953.

Hamm, Victor M. "Mr. Lewis in Perelandra," *Thought: Fordham University Quarterly,* XX (June, 1945), 271-90.

Harrison, Charles T. "The Renaissance Epitomized," *Sewanee Review,* LXIII (Winter, 1955), 153-61.

Hoffman, James W. "A Christian in Spite of Himself," *Presbyterian Life,* IX (February 4, 1956), 10-11, 28.

Joad, C. E. M. "Mr. Lewis's Devil," *The New Statesman and Nation,* XXIII (May 16, 1942), 324.

Kelly, Thomas R. *A Testament of Devotion.* New York: Harper, 1941.

Lee, E. George. *C. S. Lewis and Some Modern Theologians.* London: The Lindsey Press, 1944.

MacDonald, George. *The Princess and the Goblin.* New York: Macmillan, 1926.

"The Man on the Cover," *Pulpit Digest,* XXXVI (March, 1956), 22.

Myres, John L. "Miracles," *Nature,* CLX (August 30, 1947), 275-76.

Phillips, J. B. *Your God Is Too Small.* New York: Macmillan, 1955.

"The Reluctant Convert," *Time,* LXVII (February 6, 1956), 98.

Sayers, Dorothy. *The Mind of the Maker.* New York: Harcourt, Brace, 1941.

Soper, David Wesley. "Dorothy Sayers and the Christian Synthesis," *Religion in Life,* XXI (1951), 21.

Thompson, Francis. *The Hound of Heaven.* Mount Vernon, New York: Peter Pauper.

Thompson, Stith. *The Folktale.* New York: Dryden, 1946.

"Time Disciplined," *Times Literary Supplement,* No. 2773 (March 25, 1955), p. 181.

Tolkien, J. R. R. "On Fairy Stories," *Essays Presented to Charles Williams* (compiled by C. S. Lewis). London: Oxford, 1947. (Available in paperback edition. Grand Rapids, Michigan: Wm. B. Eerdmans, 1966.)

Wagner, Richard. *The Ring of the Nibelung* (translated by Margaret Armour). New York: Garden City, 1939.

Wain, John. "Pleasure, Controversy, and Scholarship," *The Spectator,* CXCIII (October 1, 1954), 403.

Walsh, Chad. "Back to Faith," *The Saturday Review of Literature,* XXXIX (March 3, 1956), 32.

———. "C. S. Lewis and the Christian Life," *Catholic World,* CLXVIII (February, 1949), 370-75.

———. "C. S. Lewis, Apostle to the Skeptics."

Atlantic Monthly, CLXXVIII (September, 1946), 115-19.

————. *C. S. Lewis, Apostle to Skeptics.* New York: Macmillan, 1949.

————. "The Pros and Cons of C. S. Lewis," *Religion in Life,* XVIII (1949), 222-28.

Williams, Charles, ed. *The Letters of Evelyn Underhill.* London: Longmans, Green, 1943.

————. *The Place of the Lion.* New York: Pellegrini and Cudahy, 1951.